The SECRETS TO HAPPY PARENTING, HAPPY KIDS

Understanding How Different Styles Affect The Development Of Your Kids

Nijel James

Copyright

Copyright © 2022

NIJEL JAMES

All rights to this book are reserved. No permission is given for any part of this book to be reproduced, transmitted in any form or means, electronic or mechanical, stored in a retrieval system, photocopied, recorded, scanned, or otherwise. Any of these actions require the proper written permission of the publisher.

Disclaimer

All knowledge contained in this book is given for informational and educational purposes only. The author is not accountable for any results or outcomes that emanate from using this material. Constructive attempts have been made to provide both accurate and effective information, but the author is not bound for the accuracy or use/misuse of this information.

A word from the Author

Before I became a parent, I had a lot of misconceptions about how to properly care for a baby. I had seen my mother do many things one way, and assumed that she knew best. When my first child was born, I didn't think much about what I would or should do differently. That was until I saw my sister in-law doing stuff a lot differently that really worked so much better. Her kids were less cranky, and she seemed a lot happier. Soon after, I watched other mothers with their kids and realized they were doing things that were so much more effective. I asked around a lot, read lots of books and articles, listened to the advice of other parents, talked with friends and family members who I respected, did lots of experimenting on my own children, etc... until finally things started to fall into place for me.

For me, parenting was one of those things I learnt on the job. My 'dad senses' didn't seem to kick in until I had been a parent for a while. As I watched other parents, they taught me what worked and what didn't. When I was in the midst of a frustrating toddler phase, I would ask myself how things were done by my friends and see if it was any better or different. It wasn't my instinctive desire to have my kid act like every other kid out there that made me do it that way, but more so that it just seemed like the best way to parent from as many angles of experience as possible.

I read lots of books on parenting - from the classics to the more current sources. I'm writing this book as I've realized that having a kid is like being on a long road trip through a country you've never visited before. You're going to have to look at the map from time to time to make sure you're going in the right direction, but more often than not, you'll find yourself wandering around aimlessly until your instincts kick in.

Even the best of the best baby experts can only tell us what works for other people's babies. All those baby books are just one perspective of many different approaches parents take with their kids. The techniques in this book have worked for me and have been proven to work by other parents who have gone before me (and please remember that any such "proven" techniques may not work for you). Not all techniques in this book will work as well for you as they do for me, but I hope you will find something that does.

I hope you pick up on them and use them as much as possible to help ease the transition from child to parent.

Thanks for reading!

Nigel James

About the Author

Nijel James is a father to two amazing kids. He's been practicing different parenting philosophies for over 15 years and has watched children change from chubby babies to hyper kids to teenagers. He's seen it all and has learned how to deal with that change - by asking *"What makes me happy? What makes my child happy? How can I make both of us happier?"*

Nijel writes regularly about parenting, education, and the challenges of being a Dad! He's passionate about helping other parents improve the way they parent their kids.

Who is this book for?

1. Soon to be parents

As you're about to bring a new life into this world, you're going to have a lot of questions. Some things that might concern you include:

- When should my child eat certain foods?
- How do I get my toddler to go to bed without a fuss?
- How do I feed a toddler who spits up often?
- How do I deal with tantrums or meltdowns?
- How to stop my child from being bossy!
- When should I start potty training my toddler?

2. Current parents

Your toddler/baby is about to enter a different world. She might be going to school, making new friends, and starting complex tasks that are beyond her control. You're going to want to know:

- How do I get my teen to do their homework?
- How can I keep my teen from bullying their classmates?

3. Anyone with kids or teenagers in their lives!

This book isn't just for parents of single-digit year olds. It's for everyone! You'll find answers to nagging questions such as:

- How can I give my son something productive to do during the summer break?

- What kind of punishment is best for my daughter when she breaks a rule?

- How can I get my kid to exercise regularly?

4. Anyone on the ready-to-parent spectrum!

Although this book is written with a preschooler in mind (as are most parenting books), most of the ideas in this book can work well with younger children, teenagers and even adults!

Parenting isn't just about avoiding the crazy tantrums that can derail a day. It's about preventing them from ever happening in the first place!

What you'll learn in the book

• Recognizing the five parenting styles that influence you and your child's behavior

• What to do when you disagree with your child or feel frustrated

• How to set and enforce limits, create a loving relationship, handle sensitive topics, deal with tantrums and more

• How children learn from their parents and what this means for your relationship

• How to build an effective communication pattern starting today so that you can resolve conflicts quickly and effectively

• How to build an effective way of communicating emotions in both yourself and your child

• How to build trust and a relationship that can be there for the long-term

• How to create the climate that encourages your child's happiness, self-esteem and intelligence

• How to go beyond just teaching your child new skills and establish a relationship based on emotional security and trust that they will go their own way while you go yours

This book can help teach parents how to reach out to other parents in similar situations, compare notes with other parents of other ages, learn different parenting methods, decide what would work best for them given their child's ages, establish a relationship with each other, reach out to others in similar situations or just enjoy reading from someone who has such a good understanding of this subject matter. It will help parents who are unsure where to start, what parenting methods to try, or have experienced problems in their relationship with their child.

The Eureka Moment

I never thought I was doing a bad job as a parent until I realized that I was doing to my kids what my parents did to me. When I would get home from a long day, they would want their daddy, they wanted me to play with them and to be their friend. Without even knowing it, I had adopted an authoritarian parenting style where I focused on making rules and keeping the peace. In hindsight, maybe I was strict so that I could have some "me" time. I overheard my daughter saying to her little brother, "Dad only likes us when we are good."

I sympathized with my kids because I too often felt like my parents didn't care about me unless I was doing what they wanted. I realized that the root cause of their problem came from not having enough face time with me. It was a simple fix but one that requires a paradigm shift in parenting. I needed to let them see me as a dad, not as the father or the boss.

The results were amazing: no more lying or fighting and now they are opening up to me about how they feel and making it easier for me to see where things might need attention.

In this book, you will see how to break out of the mold and how to become a great parent again. You will see how to end the pain that you are feeling as a parent and learn about the other choices available for effective parenting.

If I could go back, I would tell myself this:

"James, you are a great parent. You are showing your children what a good parent looks like. Of course they will want to be with

you when they get home from school and from sports, but you also need to make it a priority to let them see you as their dad."

Regardless of where you are in your parenting journey, I strongly encourage you to read this book to learn how to become a great parent again.

Contents

Copyright 2
Disclaimer 3
A word from the Author 4
About the Author 6
Who is this book for? 7
   1. Soon to be parents 7
   2. Current parents 7
   3. Anyone with kids or teenagers in their lives! 7
   4. Anyone on the ready-to-parent spectrum! 8
What you'll learn in the book 9
The Eureka Moment 11
Introduction 18
Chapter 1: What parenting is and what it isn't 22
   What Is Parenting? 22
   What parenting isn't 23
   How you'll cope with the changes 25
   Key takeaway 31
Chapter 2: Parenting Styles 32
   Uninvolved Parenting 32
   Authoritarian Parenting 34
   Permissive Parenting 35
   Authoritative Parenting 35
   How Each Style Affects Your Child 36

Key Takeaway 39
Chapter 3: Why Your Child Behaves the Way They Do 40
   What Causes a Child to Behave the Way They Do? 40
   Reasons for Misbehavior 41
   Encouraging Good Behavior... 43
   The Secret To Raising A Well-Behaved Child...................... 44
   Show them affection 46
   Features of Temperament 48
   Activeness.. 48
   Regularity... 48
   Approach and withdrawal: 49
   Adjustment to Change: 49
   Mood: 49
   Attentiveness.. 49
   Key Takeaway 49
Chapter 4: What Parent Are You? 50
   The Positive Parent 50
   Raising a happy child... 52
   The Don'ts of Raising a Happy Child 54
   Bonding Activities for Parents and Children 56
Chapter 5: Warmth and Nurturance 61
   What is Parental Warmth? 61
   The Essence of Parental Warmth 62
   Parenting with a Sense of Humor 64
   Extrinsic Motivation 66

Intrinsic Motivation 67
How Do You Help a Child Develop Motivation? 68
Motivating Your Children 70
Key Takeaway 70

Chapter 6: Of Boundaries and Limits 71
When Boundaries are Needed 71
The Essence of Parental Boundaries 73
Know Where to Draw the Limit 76

Chapter 7: Balancing Parenting, Work and Life 81
Coping with Stress 81
Routines to Make 85
Designating Approved Activities 86

Chapter 8: Building Effective Communication 90
Understanding Your Child's Love Language 91
Physical Contact 91
How You Can Encourage Family Discussion 96
Leverage the Power of Listening 97
Use a Word of Caution 98
Handling Serious and Important Discussion 100
Key Takeaway 100

Chapter 9: Building the Emotions 101
Pay Attention to Your Emotions 102
Helping Your Children Grow Emotionally 102
Be Mindful of Their Emotions 103
Label Your Child's Feelings 103

Guiding Children as They Identify Feelings 104
Calming an Anxious Child..105
Parenting an Angry Child 107
Address the Behavior, Not the Emotion 108
Motivating A Sad Child 109

Chapter 10: Building Self-Esteem 111
Building the Courage 111
Developing Empathy 113
Milestones in Empathy 114
Killing the Mentality of Being a Victim 115
Helping a Child with a Victim Mentality 117
Key Takeaway 119

Chapter 11: Reward and Punishment 120
Using Rewards to Motivate 120
Rewarding Behavior 121
Why Incentive-Based Parenting is a Bad Idea............122
Create a Productivity Routine 124
Applying Proper Sanctioning......................................125

Chapter 12: Knowing the Difference Between Responsibility, Choice, and Freedom 129
Teaching Children to be Responsible 129
How to Give Children Freedom..................................130
Giving Freedom Without Undermining Parental Authority 134
Tips for Setting Boundaries 135

Key Takeaway 137
Conclusion 138

Introduction

When I was a kid, a friend told me that in their house it was mandatory to go to bed at 9pm. It was a rule everyone in his household had to follow. He told me that he was once made fun of by some of our classmates when he revealed that it is normal for children to sleep by 9 p.m. They usually go to bed whenever they want; their parents didn't tell them what to do. He was taken aback and wondered what kind of parents they had and why his parents approached the same situation in such a different way. I was surprised and wondered what kinds of parents mine were and why our parents treated the same situation with a different approach. You may be familiar with that story because it had happened to almost every one of us as a kid. However, you noticed that your parents raised you differently from your friends' parents raised them.

Have you observed that the way our parents raised us determines how we turned out to be in most cases? Most times, we are a reflection of our childhood and background. We have seen children whose parents have helped them to become something great in life, and we have seen children whose lives are nothing to write home about because of the way their parents raised them. What a child becomes is mostly determined by how that child is raised? That is why the matters relating to Parenting should not be taken with levity.

As parents and intending parents, I can say that the future of your children is in your hands. Yes, I know children must play their roles in their success stories, but you are responsible for molding them into who they become. Am I saying children should not take responsibility for their actions as they grow? No. I am only saying that children turned out to be the way you raised them most often than not. Some children are confident and intelligent, while some children have low self-esteem. Some children can make intelligent decisions independently, while others base their decisions on what their friends say. This difference is often because their parents raise them with different parenting styles.

You may want to ask why parents have different parenting styles. Well, some imitate the parenting style of their parents. They want to raise their children the way they have been raised. Some choose their parenting style based on information gathered from different sources like books, social media, the internet, etc. That is why it is important to read good books on Parenting like the one you are reading now. Some parents raise their kids based on their general attitude, influenced by their beliefs, feelings, and thoughts.

Culture also has a significant influence on parenting styles. What is acceptable in my culture may be taboo in your culture. How various cultures define good morals and values may differ from one another. For example, Indian parents who live in the USA may consciously or unconsciously want to imbibe their Indianian culture into their children, which may pose a major challenge. It could be more challenging when two parents from different cultural backgrounds are raising children together. For instance, my wife and I faced some challenges in the early years of raising our kids because she is Korean. We saw things from different perspectives. For instance, my wife is very conservative about children's clothing style and body decorations which I was liberal about. Her definition of respect was different from mine. She believes there are unique ways to serve elders food and drink. Many more cultural differences were a challenge until we did the needful-agreeing on our parenting styles.

Do you know that most times, parents choose some parenting style unintentionally? When you ask them why they do some things in relation to their children, they find it hard to give you a reasonable answer. When raising your child, you should not base your decision on trial and error. Parents and intending parents should be more intentional about raising their children.

The early years are the molding stage that should be taken seriously. Like in a computer, garbage in, garbage out; it is what you put into your children that they give back to you and the society. If you see people behaving unruly, it could be traced to their upbringing. If you see people who don't like to express themselves, you could trace it to their upbringing. Most often than not, our society reflects the parenting style that was used to raise every one of us. Parenting styles could affect a child's confidence, morals, and perspectives. Therefore, it is important to apply a healthy parenting style for a child's growth and development. How you discipline and relate with your children will influence them till adulthood.

Before choosing a parenting style to adopt in raising your kids, you have to know the different parenting styles and how they affect kids. Majorly, we have permissive, authoritative, neglectful, and authoritarian parenting styles. Every of these parenting styles has its effect on children. The difference and uniqueness of these parenting styles will be discussed as you read this book. The parenting style used may also differ from child to child, and that's why you need to understudy your child before you can decide the parenting method that will be most healthy and effective. Each parenting style may be useful in specific situations in a child, and that is why you must understand the various parenting styles before adopting them for your child.

To be happy as a parent at your old age, your children have to be happy. For your children to live happily in life, you have to strive to raise them as best as possible. After you have raised your children, will they be glad to say that they are proud of their parents, or would they hiss and wish they had other parents? Will you look back when you become a grandparent and applaud yourself for how you have raised your kids?

I do not mean to scare you; good parenting is possible if you have and apply the right knowledge. I will take you through the different parenting styles and apply them in raising your children. So, relax and sip your tea as I take you through the journey of becoming a happy parent with happy kids.

Chapter 1: What parenting is and what it isn't

Parenting is a term that every parent thinks they know and understand, but many know nothing or little about it in the real sense. I was at an event when a lady and I started talking about Parenting, and I was shocked at her understanding of Parenting. She was saying that Parenting is about waking up early, preparing the kids for school, and making sure they look good. Wow! Is that all there is to Parenting? NO! To effectively parent a child, you need to understand Parenting and not assume that you know all there is because you have children.

Most times, people are happy when they are expecting a baby, and they begin to ask various questions like, "How do I properly breastfeed a baby? How can I choose a good school for my child? What are the best foods to give babies?" and many other questions. While those questions are good, often, parents don't remember to ask questions about Parenting and what it takes to be a good parent. You need to understand what Parenting entails to know the best approach to raise your kids.

<u>What Is Parenting?</u>

Parenting means supporting and enhancing a child's intellectual, emotional, social, and physical development from childhood to adulthood. Parenting does not involve biological parents alone but includes anyone who is the child's caretaker. The caretaker could be family members or non-family if the child is adopted, in an orphanage, or brought up in foster care. In other words, anyone can be a 'parent' once they are in charge of raising a child.

From the definition of Parenting above, you observe that Parenting is not limited to the physical wellbeing of a child; it also involves the child's intellectual, emotional, and social development. Most times, people focus on the physical aspects by ensuring that they feed and clothe well; and the intellectual development by sending their children to good schools. However, people tend to forget about a child's social and emotional development because they don't know that those aspects are equally important in a child's life.

What parenting isn't

There are various misconceptions many have about Parenting. One of them includes what we discussed above: Parenting is not limited to biological parents alone but anyone in charge of raising a child. In addition, there are other misconceptions about Parenting that you should know about to raise a child successfully.

Myth 1

Many believe that Parenting is natural and does not need to be learned. That is a great misconception that has caused many to raise their children improperly. Parenting, like any other thing, can be learned. You don't make a good parent by just spontaneously doing things. To raise a child well, you have to understand the reason for your every action. We have many parents with bad parenting skills because they think they can raise a child the way they feel. You successfully parent a child by just the way you feel. You have to parent a child the proper way. When raising your child, your feelings can betray you, but knowledge will help you make the right decisions when your feelings have failed you.

Myth 2

Good parents never get angry. If you agree to that statement, you are among those who believe in that misconception. Good parents have emotions; they can be happy, sad, surprised, or angry. Anger is one of the emotions that anyone can express. It is not a crime for a parent to get angry at situations. What matters is how that anger is controlled or managed. Parents should be free to share their feelings in a way that won't have a negative impact on their children. You may want to ask how you will do that; don't worry, you will learn about that as we proceed.

Myth 3

Another misconception is that parents should always reward their children for doing things right. Rewarding your child always for doing things right indirectly teaches the child that everything should be done for reward. Rewarding your child for doing things right could be once in a while, but you shouldn't make it a norm to reward them for doing things right. Your child won't understand the value of what they are doing when you always reward them. You take their eyes away from the values and importance of that thing to the rewards they will get.

Myth 4

Some parents believe they have to raise their children the same way they were raised. That is a misconception that has led many to raise their children inappropriately. You shouldn't do things because your parents did it; you should do things because they are right. Your parents could be wrong in their approach to raising you, so you don't have to use that same approach for your children. I am not saying you cannot emulate your parents if they applied the right method in raising you. I am only saying that you can do better if your parents made some mistakes in raising you.

You shouldn't repeat your parents' mistakes in raising your child because you want to follow in their footsteps.

Myth 5

I have seen many parents who feel they can never be wrong when dealing with their children. But unfortunately, you cannot always be proper no matter who you are. Sometimes, you make mistakes, and you should learn to accept that. When you make mistakes, try to accept, and correct them rather than prove a point.

Myth 6

Another common misconception about Parenting is that Parenting is one-sided. Parenting is not one-sided; it should involve both the father and mother. Most times, raising a child has been made the mother's responsibility alone. The raising of a child should be by both parents except in special cases and circumstances where one of the parents is unavoidably unavailable.

How you'll cope with the changes

Unarguably, Parenting comes with new demands, and everything else that comes with it can be stressful, especially if it's your first time being a parent. Being a parent means that you are responsible for someone else, and you know that you cannot afford to fail at it. You can spend the entire day at your 9-5 job, and just when you want to relax, your kids need attention. So you struggle to make yourself available and try to be the best parent you could be. Sometimes, you mess things up when things get beyond your control. When things don't go as planned, you may begin to feel worried, unhappy, tense, frustrated, and stressed. Things like that are normal because parenthood is a new phase that you have not been used to. You have spent at least your first eighteen years on your own without having to look after anyone, and then you have the responsibility to shape a child's life to be a responsible adult in the future.

To parent a child successfully, you need to learn how to cope with parenthood changes. Understanding that such changes are inevitable and managing them makes the difference between successful and unsuccessful parents. If you don't manage the changes well, you could become a harsh, irrational, angry, bitter, and sad parent that no child can relate with.

No matter the changes you are going through, there are some things you can do that will help you to cope with those changes. I have explained some things that will help you cope with these changes below.

Make Time for Yourself

You will always have something to do for the kids almost every time. If you are not conscious about making time for yourself, you will discover that you have spent your entire life living for your kids. Taking care of your kids is important, but that should not stop you from taking care of yourself mentally or emotionally. You can spend thirty minutes in a day to what you enjoy doing. That helps you get some things off your mind and catch some breath. You can choose to have your bath, watch TV, read or book or whatever helps you to relax. Yes, I know there are house chores and other things to attend to but kindly ignore them; they can wait. The time you spend with yourself is important as the time spent with the kids.

Get Help

Sometimes, you need help to attend to some things in the home. Instead of engulfing yourself with the responsibility of attending to everything in the home, you can issue some out to people that can assist you. Your stress can be reduced when you get help because you cannot always do everything yourself.

Relax

As much as you want to be a good parent, know that you are bound to make mistakes. Don't beat yourself up for making mistakes. Instead, relax and seek ways you can be better. Parenting is not a military role so, don't treat it as one. Relax and work things out bit by bit.

Spend Time with Your Partner

If you have a partner, spend time with them. Some parents grow apart because they have channeled all their energy into their children. Spending time with your partner, hearing sweet words, feeling their physical touch can help you get matters off your mind and relax.

Talk to Other Parents

You will think you are the only one facing problems in Parenting until you talk to other parents. Talking to other parents helps you learn about new strategies to overcome challenges. Some things may not work out well because you don't know how to do them. So, talking to other parents can help reduce the stress of figuring it out all by yourself.

Express Yourself

You can get some things off your mind when you talk to someone about it. I am not saying you should tell everyone what you are passing through, but you can express your feelings once in a while. You can talk to your friend, spouse, parent, or colleague. Sometimes, all you need to get over the tension is a word of encouragement from someone and a pat on your shoulder.

Inculcating the Right Attitude

No matter your child's age range, you will agree with me that Parenting is challenging. It could be amazing this minute and then frustration in the next. "How can I stop my children from fighting? How can I make my baby eat well? How can I get my kids to sleep early?" These and many more are the questions we seek answers to on our minds. Most times, we are looking for strategies to change our children's attitude; by making them fit into what works for us. But unfortunately, this method usually doesn't work but only complicates the situation.

We need to stop changing our children and then focus on changing ourselves first. Some of the attitudes we are trying to change in our children may be due to our attitudes, parenting styles, and principles (don't worry; we will talk about that in the next chapter). Parenting is not a war front so, stop taking everything seriously. Instead, we can change our perspective about parenting challenges, take things easier on ourselves and be a parent with the right attitude. By making some changes in our attitude, we will enjoy our kids more, and our kids' behavior will begin to align with ours. Some changes you can make in your attitude that will help yield positive attitudes in your children are listed below.

Lower your expectations

You need to remember that your children are children. Sometimes, you expect much from your children, forgetting that they are just kids. When you expect too much from your kids, they are most likely to fail, and you only increase your chances of getting disappointed and frustrated. Training your children about 'adult" behavior is good, but lower your expectations and remember that they can make mistakes.

Remember That the Challenges Are Temporary

When you first gave birth, waking up early, sleeping late, and feeding a baby at intervals seemed like forever. That phase or challenge ended after some time, so is every challenge you may face in your parenthood. Know that every phase will pass, so just take it easy on yourself.

Raise the Child You Have

Most parents have a picture of the child they want even before the child's arrival. Some want a dancer, athlete, musician, or even a genius. Forget about what you want the child to be and focus on who the child is at the moment. If you have more than a child, you need to focus on each child individually. Your children are different from each other, so stop comparing them. Their flaws, personalities, strengths, weaknesses, and qualities differ, so they should be parented in ways unique to them. When you focus on parenting the child you have, it is easier for your job as a parent.

Connect with Your Child

Children connected with their parents exhibit a more positive attitude than those who don't. Connecting with your children makes Parenting easier because they listen more and feel less tense. Try to connect with your child first whenever they exhibit bad behavior before addressing the behavior. Your child may exhibit some negative behavior, such as a need for a feeling of isolation or the need for attention. Spend time with your children other than discipline. Play games, go out and have a nice time with them. By doing that, they tend to listen more to you and will imbibe the values you want to share with them.

Know Your Parenting Style

Parenting styles are the strategies that parents use to raise their kids. They also involve discipline styles parents use to impose their expectations. Parenting styles differ from one parent to another. While some are authoritative, some are flexible and don't take things rigidly. For example, when you were a kid, you remember how what works in your family doesn't work in your friend's family. That is because individual parents applied different parenting styles in raising their children. To raise a kid successfully, you need to know the different parenting styles and apply them in raising children. I will see you in the next chapter, where we extensively discuss the various parenting styles.

In conclusion, there is more to Parenting than just paying the fees, feeding the kids, and getting them ready for school. Parenting also involves developing a child socially, emotionally, and intellectually. Unfortunately, there are many myths about Parenting that have caused many to be unsuccessful in raising their kids. Parenthood is a different phase that comes with challenges, so it is best to learn how to cope with the changes that come with Parenting. When raising a child, we often focus on changing the child's behaviors rather than looking at what we have not been doing right. To see the desired changes in your child, learn how to maintain the right attitude, and you will be surprised that the changes you desire will happen easier than you expected.

Key takeaway

Parenting is not limited to biological parents alone but includes anyone who is the child's caretaker.

Chapter 2: Parenting Styles

In the first chapter, we discussed the basic things you need to know about Parenting, understanding how to cope with changes, infixing the right attitude, and identifying your parenting style to guide you in raising your kids appropriately. In this chapter, we will be discussing the different parenting styles you need to know to be aware of which category you fall into and make the correct adjustment.

Each child is unique with their strengths and weaknesses and therefore requires different styles to handle them to become useful to themselves and their society. While there is no specific manual for Parenting, it is considered one of the most challenging tasks in life. Most parents struggle to determine the appropriate style to raise their children to become well-rounded, mentally strong, and successful in life. For example, some parents create a good rapport with their children and train them to talk about different subjects. In contrast, some other parents are strict and unapproachable, creating a communication barrier between them and their kids. You might have asked yourself the question, "what parent am I, or perhaps what parent do I want to be?" I will help take you through the different parenting styles you should know.

The four types of parenting styles used in child psychology are: Uninvolved, Authoritarian, Permissive, Authoritative.

Let's have an extensive discussion on each of them to know how they can affect your upbringing.

Uninvolved Parenting

Do you find any of these statements familiar?

- You don't ask your kid what they were taught in school, let alone ask if they were given homework.
- You are always engrossed with your job and do not have spare time for your kids.
- You don't care who your kid's friends are
- You don't care about your kid's hobbies or interest
- You don't even know when they are going through stuff
- You can't even say for sure who your kids are.

If any of those questions sound familiar to you, you might be an uninvolved parent. Uninvolved parents usually don't meet the needs of their kids, both physical and emotional needs, and provide little to no supervision. Uninvolved parents act emotionally distant from their kids and have little or no knowledge about their kids' development. They show little love, warmth, and attention towards their kids. In many cases, kids with such parents receive no nurturing, parental attention, or even guidance, and as such, they suffer low self-esteem over time. Most of the time, uninvolved parents are neglective, and it is always not deliberate; it may be a result of parental stress and experience. Sometimes, these parents forget that their kids are dependent on them for almost everything, but they tend to leave them to cater to themselves like an adult. For uninvolved parents with infants, they may not meet their basic needs such as food, shelter, and sleep. For toddlers, it could mean not modeling their behaviors in the presence of their kids, not caring about people that move around their kids, not screening TV shows or programs, etc. In addition, several uninvolved parents are usually overwhelmed with many difficult situations like mental illnesses, drug abuse, or even work and paying outrageous bills. Most of the mentioned problems do not allow most parents to care for their kids. Often, kids with uninvolved parents exhibit some behavioral problems, perform poorly in school, and withdraw from other kids.

Authoritarian Parenting

Do you find any of these statements familiar?

- You believe you should always impose rules on your kids.
- You feel what your kid wants doesn't matter, and you need to be the one to choose for them constantly.
- You believe your kids should be seen but not heard.

The word authoritarian depicts a strict approach to raising your kids. If any of the above questions sound familiar to you, you might be an authoritarian parent. Authoritarian parents would give directions, use discipline, and set firm rules but may not give their kids the opportunity to share their views or perspectives. Obedience is their watchword for an authoritarian parent, and they usually establish and follow through with consequences. They usually wouldn't permit their kids to be involved in problem-solving obstacles or challenges as they always want to be in charge. Parents who are authoritarians prefer punishments to discipline. Thus, their style doesn't expose the children to making better choices. Instead, they train their kids to feel remorseful and apologize for their mistakes. Most of the time, communication is a one-way thing from parent to child with no particular explanations for their rules. Authoritarian parents are typically less nurturing with limited flexibility. Authoritarian parents who have infants might not set strict rules initially but could create high rigid sleeping and feeding schedules for their kids.

Permissive Parenting

Do you find any of these statements familiar?

- You set rules but become very reluctant to impose limits.
- You believe kids should have the freedom to experiment with different things.
- You feel your kids will learn from their own experiences and that you don't need to interfere in their life.

If any of the above questions sound familiar to you, you might be a permissive parent. Permissive parents tend to take up the role of a friend in their kids' life rather than the parenting role. They exhibit low demand from their kids and high responsiveness. The permissive parents are very lenient; they avoid conflict and often listen to their kids' plea at the first call to distress. Usually, they do not put in much effort to discourage their kid's bad behaviors or poor habits. Instead, they put in great effort to ensure that their kids are happy, and that could even be at their own expense. Kids with permissive parents have a lot of freedom, and they are not always well monitored. Kids often have little to no responsibility or chores, and they usually have no well-structured day. Permissive parents with infants and toddlers don't often set a scheduled sleeping and feeding time and often eat, sleep or do other things whenever they feel like it.

Authoritative Parenting

Do you find any of these statements familiar?

- You set rules and give the reasons behind them.
- You do everything possible to maintain a good relationship with your kids.

- You always put your kids' feelings into consideration despite setting out strict guidelines for them.

If any of the above questions sound familiar to you, you might be an authoritative parent. An authoritative parent sets rules and consequences and considers their kids' opinions. As much as these parents believe they are in charge, they frequently communicate and believe that their kids' opinions matter and validate their feelings. Authoritative parents put in all the time and energy to prevent bad behaviors in their kids before they start. Also, they use positive discipline strategies to instill good behaviors in their kids. For example, they use a reward and praise system to encourage their kids to do well. Discipline is usually instilled in kids to guide and coach logical and natural consequences. According to researchers, kids with authoritative parents tend to do excellently well and grow to become responsible adults. In addition, their kids find it very easy and comfortable to express their opinion, make good decisions and have the initiative to evaluate safety risks by themselves. Authoritative parents who have infants may set a feeding and sleeping time for them, but they wouldn't hesitate to make the necessary adjustments to suit their babies better. Those of them who have toddlers wouldn't permit their kids to stay up watching TV when it is bedtime, and they wouldn't handle their kids' health and safety in an unserious manner.

How Each Style Affects Your Child

Raising and caring for children is one of the most important activities anyone could think of. It is incredibly challenging and, at the same rewarding. The way a parent brings up their children will reflect when they grow into adulthood. Similarly, how parents interact and discipline their kids greatly influences them throughout their lifetime. As a parent, you need to understand how your parenting style affects your kid's growth, development, and health. Let's dive into how different styles of Parenting affect the children to help guide you to become the parent you would like to be.

Uninvolved Parenting

Most experts have concluded that kids with uninvolved parents have severe problems in nearly every area of their lives. Kids of uninvolved parents lag in cognition, social skills, and emotional skills. In addition, they find it difficult to behave well as they were not taught how to set boundaries at home. Usually, such children end up having low self-esteem such that they tend not to trust anyone and have unhealthy relationships with people.

Authoritarian Parenting

Since authoritarian parents are strict and want their children to obey all rules irrespective of how it affects them, they tend to pay the price for their lapses. Their children's opinions do not count and are not always valued; thus, their kids usually have a higher risk of low self-esteem. As a result, the children become unnecessarily aggressive and hostile, disrupting their thought processes. When they need to think about making headway in the future, they will focus on their anger towards their children. Even though authoritarian parents put in all the effort to instill discipline in their children, their kids are terrible liars to avoid their punishments.

Permissive Parenting

Kids with permissive parents often exhibit behavioral problems as they may never adhere to rules and authority. In most cases, such kids struggle in their academics. In addition, since their parents are free thinkers and wouldn't stress to enforce good habits, kids with permissible parents suffer several health problems. For example, they are prone to being obese as their parents struggle to curtail what they eat (junk food). Some even have dental cavities as their parents would not enforce good habits like brushing their teeth. Finally, most kids with permissive parents are free to speak out their minds. Though this allows them to express their creative side, they are likely unable to understand boundaries even when they are far from home.

Authoritative Parenting

Authoritative Parenting is considered the healthiest approach for kids by psychologists worldwide. It is the most celebrated parenting style, and it's difficult to point out its drawbacks. This parenting style finds the balance between two alternatives, the best to raise kids. It is not easy to achieve a balance of discipline and freedom for kids; thus, this parenting style is lengthy and challenging to implement. Rebellion is a natural part of childhood, so kids might become naturally rebellious and angry. Authoritative parents may become frustrated when their kids become rebellious. They usually have high expectations and expend all their time and energy to raise their kids the right way.

Children of authoritarian parents tend to be more concerned about their actions per time; thus, they become somewhat restricted in thoughts and not likely to make impulsive choices. Usually, kids with authoritarian parents tend to be disciplined, self-motivated, independent, and very bright academically. But experts have shown that the overly rigid approach pressurizes the children to attain perfection and, in turn, exposes them to internalizing behaviors like being timid and withdrawn.

Children with authoritative parents are more likely to become self-reliant, socially accepted, well-behaved, and independent adults. It is rare to find reports about anxiety and depression for such kids. Similarly, they likely wouldn't indulge in drugs or antisocial behaviors.

Key Takeaway

There is no manual to Parenting, and you should know that different things work for different people. As such, it is always good to remember that it is whatever works best for your kids that you should put to use. In other words, you could act as a permissible parent at a point and then, depending on the situation, switch to becoming an authoritative parent. It isn't easy to be consistent, but you can try as much as possible to attain a balance. It is not helpful to engage in guilt or shame as a parent. Authoritative Parenting considered the best style so far, so you can embrace this style if you make a conscious effort. You can always have a healthy and positive relationship with your children and still establish authority over them in a good way. And in a matter of time, it will reflect in your kids as it would help them stand out among their peers.

Chapter 3: Why Your Child Behaves the Way They Do

In the previous chapter, we discussed the different parenting styles and how each of these styles affects your child. At this point, you should be able to know what type of parent you are or what type of parent you want to become and work towards raising your kids to become responsible adults. In this chapter, you will understand what drives your kids to behave the way they do, how you can encourage your kids to behave positively, understand the secrets to raising a well-behaved child, and also understand your kid's temperament.

<u>What Causes a Child to Behave the Way They Do?</u>

At one time or another, children misbehave. You can always correct your kid's bad behavior by making an effort to know why they misbehave. When you understand why kids behave the way they do, you will understand how to respond and intervene. Due to the following factors, kids behave the way they do:

Developmental factor: This can contribute to unwanted behaviors in kids. Kids tend to behave differently due to some significant events in their life or from their past experiences.

Ecological factor: Kids are often influenced by what goes on in their surroundings. For example, their home, neighborhood, friends, peers, school activities, climate, and socio-economic conditions.

External Environment: Children who grew up in a chaotic household are likely to have behavioral issues. For example, a child raised on a housing project, for example, is more likely to have a higher level of health problems. If their parents/guardians are unemployed or do not have higher earnings, they will most likely buy cheap, low-quality foods that are less nutritious but easier to prepare, potentially leading to health problems. This could lead to children and families accepting lower expectations. Children who have behavioral disorders exhibit a wide range of behaviors. Kicking, screaming, throwing objects, spitting, self-harm, aggression toward others, fighting, and crying are examples of externalizing behaviors.

Reasons for Misbehavior

Have you ever imagined why kids misbehave? If you can know why they misbehave, you'd be able to solve behavioral problems. Kids use their behavior to express how they feel about things. They often may not know how to verbalize what they think, so their behavior is their best means of communication. When your kids violate any rule you set, try something different to solve the problem and to spend more time to figure out why they misbehave.

Let's take a look at the reasons why kids misbehave:

1. They want you to meet a real need: Kids do not know enough vocabulary to express their thoughts and feelings; thus, they may not know how to communicate their needs directly to you. They might be bored, hungry, tired, or pressed. If you see that your child is hungry, then give him food. If he is tired, then let him rest. Knowing what they need at that time and helping them to curb bad behaviors. These tricks work well, and children can put up their best behaviors with them.

2. Imitating other people: kids learn behaviors by watching others; they repeat what they see. It could be watching their peers

in school, their neighbors at home, or from TV programs and videos. You can restrict them from watching certain programs, playing odd video games, or any manner of activities that could disrupt their behavior.

3. They crave attention: a child might exhibit attention-seeking behavior stemming from jealousy or loneliness. When you are with friends and family or engaged in activities, your kid might feel left out. In this case, a kid might start throwing tantrums or start misbehaving just to get your attention. Instead, spend time with your child, cuddle, read a book and talk about the day.

4. They are confused: Sometimes, a child misbehaves because he doesn't know exactly what to do at a point in time. Such a child lacks the skills and practicality to solving problems. For example, a child might hit another child because he wants the chocolate in his hand. You need to teach your kids what to do instead of giving them consequences for their behavior.

5. To show that they can also be in Charge: Kids tend to misbehave to say that they can't be forced to do things they don't want to do. Teens especially may become rebellious to show that they can also make their own choices. So you can give your kids the privilege to do things they are interested in after they might have done their chores.

6. To test boundaries: Kids are very daring and would often test you to know if you mean what you have said. They want to know the consequence of breaking the rules you set and confirm if you were serious about it. You need to always be consistent, set the rules, and never hesitate to inform them about the consequences attached.

7. Mental Issues: Sometimes, children don't misbehave out of the will, but they could be dealing with underlying mental health

issues that you may not know if you do not pay keen attention. Some kids are bullied by their fellow students or even treated unwholesomely by their teachers. As a result, they may end up being anxious and depressed. In that case, see your child's pediatrician or consult a trained mental health professional to confirm if they don't have any underlying emotional issues that might contribute to their behavioral problems.

Encouraging Good Behavior

Set the pace for them to follow: Children often learn by examples, and it is easy for them to pick up some social habits by picking people's behavior around them. Thus, if you want your children to behave responsibly, you need to make them see you as their role model and act by example. Teach your kids how to take care of the home and do the house chores appropriately.

Say what you mean: When you abide by your promises, whether good or bad, your children will learn to trust and respect you every time. It gives them a sense of assurance that you will never let them down or even change your mind after giving them your word. When you say you'd take them shopping during the weekend, they keep their mind fixated on your promise and patiently wait for you to fulfill it.

Celebrate Your Child's good deeds: It is very good to find natural ways to teach your child empathy. For example, anytime your child does well in school, encourage them with gifts and rewards, making them work hard to achieve more. Similarly, when your child accords due respect to older people, praise them and reinforce the child's inclination with good compliments.

The Secret To Raising A Well-Behaved Child

Every parent wants to raise a well-behaved child. After all, a kid's behavior is a reflection of their parents' skills, right? We don't want a child to bully their colleagues in school or steal materials that don't belong to them. Several parents would attest that raising a child to become responsible is hard work.

It is good to study your kids and understand their temperaments to raise them appropriately. In other words, different kids with different strokes; while some would obey rules with questions, some others would not. So let's dive into the secrets to raising a well-behaved child.

Understand Cultural Differences

In cases where parents are from different cultural backgrounds, raising a child could be challenging compared to parents with the same cultural background. The challenges are majorly because parents from different cultural backgrounds have distinct beliefs and understanding of what a well-behaved child should be. For instance, I am a Britain while my lovely wife is Korean, making it challenging to choose particular patterns for our children.

Teaching our kids how to greet was a good example of how our cultural differences played out. The Korean tradition considers greeting as a means of showing respect to those who are older. Hence, the bow serves as their means of greeting. There are, however, instances when the bow can be followed by a handshake (when it is among men). Yet, if you are shaking an older person, you have to support your right forearm with your left hand as a show of respect.

Also, for my wife, in her Korean culture, it is a thing to co-sleep with your kids. However, I strongly believe and expect that our kids ought to have their crib/bed in their own rooms and space. It is one of the best gifts I always feel I can give our kids.

Those are examples of some of our challenges until we decided that we would not allow our cultural differences to come in our way of raising our children. We communicated our differences and agreed on a common ground to raise our children. I bent to some of her ideas while she bent to some of mine. I discovered that we might not be able to achieve our goal of raising a well-behaved child if we do not let go of our ego and agree on what we both think is best for our children.

Cultural differences are a big deal when raising children and should not be taken lightly. If your spouse is someone whose cultural background is different from yours, I advise that you communicate and agree on values and beliefs to teach your children. If you teach your children something today, and your spouse teaches them something else tomorrow, you would only be at risk of the child becoming confused and ultimately not mastering any of the teachings.

An early start: sometimes, kids behave unruly without even understanding what they did wrong. For example, a kid might hit someone older than them and feel good about it if he is not corrected immediately. When you don't reprimand that kid at that early stage, putting any correction in place will become difficult when they grow older. Usually, it would seem like the right thing to such a child, and the child would become justified in his confusion. Kids take characters while growing up, so the earlier you instill discipline in them, the better. For each stage of development, there are realistic expectations for behavior. For example, a 2year old who hits somebody does not mean any harm in contrast to when an adult hits another person. Usually, such a boy might hit someone to express displeasure about something.

Now, the idea is to understand your child; it's normal for them to express their emotions, it is your responsibility to help them understand the good and bad ways of expressing them.

Be logical

Children are smart and intelligent, and most of the time, they hold you by your words. You can't possibly wake a child up from sleep today and tell her that it is bad to visit neighbors in their house and then, the next time, say that they could visit but only spend a few minutes. I mean, they aren't daft! You need to be consistent; let your no be no and yes be yes. If a child would rather prefer to eat in his room than the dining, and you believe it is neither acceptable nor good, then you have to completely refuse. If you permit such a child to eat in their room for any reason, he would believe that there is nothing wrong with such an act. For any behavior that can hurt someone or endanger anybody's life, your response should always be one, no.

Show them affection

You are like a mirror to your kids as they tend to pick up their character from you. If you keep behaving badly in the presence of your kids, don't expect them to act any way better. Therefore, you need to put up positive behaviors as it is easier to emulate you. Be devoted to your kids; always spend a good time with them as this would make them understand that you find them precious and worthwhile.

Be a role model

Gandhi said, "If you wish to change the world, be the change." Children always watch and scrutinize their caregivers. They would somehow react to what you already acted. Your actions sink deep into their subconscious state; hence, you need to be conscious about your expressions and actions around them. For example, if you want a child to treat others politely or greet people older than them, you need to also exhibit the same behavior. Similarly, if you want your child to learn how to appreciate people's kindness, you need to appreciate them when they run errands for you. You could even appreciate them with gifts and other fanciful items to appreciate them for their good conduct.

Hone Their Listening Skills

Normally kids are super-active, loud, and rowdy, and these attributes prevent them from following rules accordingly. As a parent, you need to refine your kid's listening skills to suit the behavior you want them to display. Look into their eyeballs when they speak and allow them to express their thoughts. Make sure you do not interrupt them while they speak. Though they may not find the right word to express their thoughts and feelings, be patient and allow them to speak. If your child interrupts you when you speak, do well to let him know that it is rude and remind them that you always allow them to speak freely when expressing their thoughts.

Prepare Them for Challenging Situations

You need to know how to train your children to actively tackle challenges that may come their way. For example, if you sense that your car suddenly developed a fault while taking your child to the shop, tell them what happened to the car before they find out and prepare their mind about what to expect.

Set the Rules and Consequences

There's a saying that where there is no rule, there's no sin as your child grows older, chive them more responsibility for their behavior. Also, attach consequences for unacceptable behavior so that they can consciously be in their best behavior.

Be Free with Them

Strictness doesn't guarantee that a child will turn out to be exactly what you want. Instead, apply balance and create a sense of humor. Don't be the masquerade that your child wouldn't want to face or relate freely with. Instead, tease them, laugh, join them to do what they find interesting at times, and just have fun.

Understand Child's Temperament

Have you ever asked the question about how you can understand your child's temperament? Of course, children differ; while some can be very cool, calm, and predictable, others might be difficult and not know how to express their emotions with ease.

Features of Temperament

You can only appreciate a child's uniqueness if you understand his temperament. So let's dive into the major characteristics that make up temperament.

<u>Activeness</u>: the level of a child's physical activity, restlessness, motion, and other daily activities says a lot about the child.

<u>Regularity</u>: you need to study the patterns such as sleep, appetite, bowel habits in a child. Pay attention to whether these physical functions are regular or inconsistent.

Approach and withdrawal: How does your child respond to new stimuli? You need to understand how your child reacts in places, situations, foods, and a lot more.

Adjustment to Change: You need to know if your child easily adapts to new situations and how well they can cope and adjust during this period.

Mood: Does your child have mood swings? Is he friendly at one point and turns the opposite at intervals?

Attentiveness: You need to know if your child listens and have the ability to stay on a task without any distraction

Key Takeaway

Finally, you will not make your children disciplined and responsible overnight. There would be times when kids would act rebelliously no matter how hard you try to curb them, which can be frustrating most times. But, always remember that they are kids. If you focus on the messages in this book and apply them, you will help them. And sooner, they would not even need you to teach them the right things to do as they would already know what is good and bad.

Chapter 4: What Parent Are You?

Parents have a significant influence on their children's behavior and attitudes. The way a child acts and communicates with others reflects the environment in which they were raised and how essentially, their parents raised them. Maintaining a good atmosphere at home, for example, can aid in the development of a self-assured youngster. On the other hand, a child who is anxious and nervous all of the time may be exposed to their parents' outlandish conduct frequently. As a result, it's critical to recognize that your lifestyle choices and disagreements with your partner can significantly impact your child's general development and attitude toward relationships. Overall, great Parenting and upbringing can positively impact your child's life. And it's entirely up to you as a parent to decide who your child will be and how he will develop.

The Positive Parent

Making child-rearing decisions that represent your parenting ideas and values, your child's age and stage of development, and temperament is what Positive Parenting is all about. Fostering respectful relationships based on clear expectations is at the heart of positive Parenting. Children who have a good bond with their parents are more likely to behave appropriately as adults and grow resilient, confident, caring, and responsible. In addition, positive Parenting entails being sensitive to children's particular needs and dealing with the common issues in early life with empathy and respect.

Here's an active example of positive Parenting.

Lindsey, Kelvin's 8-year-old daughter, comes to him with a dilemma. Robby, Lindsey's 10-year-old and much stronger next-door neighbor had just grabbed her ice cream cone and her change from a ten-dollar bill from the ice cream truck. Lindsey confides in her dad and he, in turn, listens to his daughter. Kelvin asks Lindsey how she wants him to deal with the matter. Lindsey tells her dad that she wants to confront Robby, but she wants him to be close by when she does so. Kelvin tells Lindsey that he thinks it's a great idea and that she should let him know when she's ready. Kelvin, however, doesn't tell Lindsey that she took money she used to get the ice cream from her piggy bank without permission, breaking a family tradition. He also doesn't tell her that getting ice cream was against his orders, which he had enforced weeks before. After several hours, Kelvin joins Lindsey in confronting Robby and demanding his ten bucks back. Robby's father, Eric overhears the talk and demands that Robby compensate Lindsey for her troubles. He also speaks with Robby and Lindsey about bullying. Kelvin returns to the house with Lindsey and expresses his admiration for her handling of the incident. Kelvin then sits down with Lindsey to talk about the two rules she disobeyed and how she can prevent making the same mistakes in the future. For breaching the rule, he adds a week of no sweets and confiscates Lindsey's ten dollars and piggy bank for a month. When sweets are allowed again two weeks later, Kelvin brings Lindsey to her favorite ice cream shop, and the two have a long conversation about the forthcoming season of their beloved football team.

Here's a step-by-step review of our active example of positive Parenting:

- Kelvin listens to Lindsey, concentrating on the issue at hand.

- Kelvin offers Lindsey his support as she handles her issue.
- Kelvin places his relationship with Lindsey, and the boy's current problem, before disciplining her for his wrongdoings.
- Kelvin doesn't ignore Lindsey's wrongdoings but points them out and talks them through with the Lindsey appropriately.
- Kelvin ensures that Lindsey experiences consequences for her behavior.
- Kelvin refocuses both of them, father and daughter, on their relationship after consequences are served.

So, how can this example be applied to positive Parenting in everyday life? We'll start by shifting our attention. We keep the end aim in mind: to assist children in developing the skills they will need to grow into healthy, thoughtful, and authentic individuals. Parents who set an excellent example for their children begin with positive Parenting as adults. Sharing your opinions and beliefs with your children is essential for positive Parenting.

<u>Raising a happy child</u>

As a parent, you should do a few things to ensure your child is properly brought up. Below are a few things you should do:

Spend Time with Each Other One-On-One

The best thing you can do to help your children develop self-confidence and healthy relationships is to spend regular quality time with them and model excellent behavior. Positive attention and emotional connection are ingrained into children's brains. When they don't get it, they seek it out negatively, resulting in power conflicts, whining, and meltdowns for parents. Taking pleasure in times of connection will also assist you in developing a deeper and more meaningful relationship.

Demonstrate Your Love for Them

All parents adore their children, yet most of them rarely show it. Parents need to demonstrate their love and affection for their children. Hugging youngsters regularly can be pretty beneficial. Simply saying "I love you" or kissing them on the cheek can brighten their day. However, keep in mind that simply expressing or showing certain things isn't enough.

Congratulate Them

Appreciate and reward your child's efforts when they do something nice. It is a significant advantage for a child. They are joyful and do not experience the sting of failure. They will improve their performance to gain more accolades. It adds to their contentment.

Show Your Appreciation for Them

Constantly show that you appreciate your kids. It will not only make them pleased but will also make them more willing to assist you. Everyone is happier when parents and children work together in the home. Children feel more connected to their parents, and parents experience more affection. The youngsters in such homes are often content. Teach your kids to appreciate what others do for them.

Negative Parenting

Negative Parenting has been debated for decades and does not appear to be going away anytime soon. Bad Parenting, as it's often known, refers to various behaviors that result in parents failing to provide appropriate direction to their children from infancy to adulthood. Children are easily influenced. They are influenced by the adults in their lives, with substantial evidence indicating their parents have the largest influence. As a result, Parenting is a duty that defines how each individual and citizen will turn out.

Negative Parenting can take several forms, as described in the preceding paragraph. It occurs when a youngster is not scolded or punished for their faults in their most basic form. On the other hand, it might occur when a youngster is subjected to excessive punishment to the point of psychological harm. Negative Parenting takes on a whole new meaning regarding child abuse.

The Don'ts of Raising a Happy Child

Every parent has a desire to raise a content, joyful, and successful child in life. Happy children are a joy to behold; their laughter and joy instantly brighten the room.

If you want to raise a happy child, you must start working right away. Some children, however, are naturally joyful while some on the other hand are not.

Don't Protect Your Kids From Failure

Allowing your child to make errors and learn from them is one of the most difficult things you can do as a parent. To assist children in preparing for inconvenient circumstances, such as conflict, struggle, and repercussions, teach them to embrace life's realities, such as conflict, struggle, and consequences. For example, allow your daughter to manage herself in the cafeteria one day if she consistently forgets to bring lunch to school. Allow her to iron out her differences with a teacher or a classmate first.

Don't Excessively Reprimand the Child

When your child makes a mistake, and you chastise or scold him excessively, it might negatively impact him. However, if your child has been honest and admitted to making a mistake, this approach may even have a much more negative impact on them.

Don't Discipline Your Public

Reprimanding, yelling, or even hitting a child in public is a sign of Bad Parenting. It will significantly negatively influence your child's self-esteem, and the humiliation associated with this kind of discipline will be difficult to overcome.

Don't Make Comparisons or Pass Judgment on Your Child

Parents must mold their children's behavior. Praise and reward them when they do well and encourage them when they don't. Try as much as possible not to compare them to their classmates. Do not chastise them because they cannot perform as well as the others. It makes a child melancholy and sad for the rest of their life. The parents' attitude and behavior determine a child's happiness or sadness. Children raised by overly critical and abusive parents often become unhappy and grumpy. Parents must instill positivism and be happy in their children early.

Don't Overindulge in Pampering

Excessive pampering of your child is not a good idea. Please don't give in to their irrational demands. Make it clear that they will not receive anything or everything they desire. Teach children that to succeed in life, they must work hard.

Do Not Always Worry About Offending Them

You may believe that your joyful child should be comfortable and free of negativity, but this is incorrect. Instead, allow your child to make mistakes and be hurt. Allowing your child to experience problems is the only way to ensure that they will be happy in the future.

Do Not Withhold Affection

Avoid withholding affection from your child. Instead, constantly show them you love and care for them. For example, if you don't often offer your child hugs or tell him or her, "I love you." Your child will feel emotionally estranged from you as a result of this.

The Relationship Between Child and Parent

The relationship between a parent and a child should promote the youngster's physical, emotional, and social growth. It's a one-of-a-kind link that every child and parent should appreciate and develop. The child's personality, life choices, and overall behavior are all shaped by this bond. It may also impact their social, physical, mental, and emotional wellbeing.

It's a fact that loving parents raise loving children. Your relationship with your children and how attached you are to them will significantly impact how they develop in the future. Young children who have a safe and healthy attachment with their parents are more likely to build happy and content relationships with others later in life. A child with a strong and loving relationship with his or her parents will learn to control his or her emotions in a stressful and tough situation. A positive parent-child relationship will also affect a child's mental, linguistic, and emotional growth.

Bonding Activities for Parents and Children

The foundation of a strong kid-parent relationship is building a relationship with your child. When there is a strong link between you and your children, they are more likely to follow the rules freely. Incorporating positive interactions into your everyday routine is one approach to enhance your bond with your children. Here are some ways to go about it.

Positively Reinforce Your Children Daily

One technique to increase parent-child bonding is to positively reinforce your children daily. It can be expressed verbally, such as "very good," or physically, like a pat on the back or an embrace. Look into what works best for the child. Early interpersonal touch is associated with later years of a child's self-esteem, life contentment, and social competence. It also has a good impact on the physical and psychological development of the child. Hug your children as soon as they wake up in the morning and before they go to bed at night, as well as often as possible throughout the day. To show them you care, rub their shoulders, establish eye contact, and stroke their backs.

Laugh Together

Parenting doesn't have to be serious all of the time. Be sure to always have a few lighter moments. It will help you create some wonderful memories.

Engage in One-On-One Communication

Take time out of your day to talk with them about their needs and how they plan to meet them. Then, every day, spend time with your child to express your love for them, play with them, and do something fun with them.

Strengthen the Link

Yes, modest actions like stroking your child's hair can help strengthen the bond. When you try to do this with teens or preteens, they usually don't enjoy it, but that's even better if you can do it with younger children. They may not be irritated and may even be content with it.

Listen Actively

Passively listening while doing your work and responding with a 'huh' or 'OK' now and then suggests that you are uninterested. Instead, stop what you're doing and listen to your child when they speak to you. Give them your undivided attention, ask them questions, and repeat what they've said. When speaking with them, remember to keep eye contact.

The early years of your relationship with your children provide the groundwork for their later years. Your child's personality will be influenced if the early parent-child bond is stressed due to numerous issues. Here are a few frequent issues that should be avoided in parent-child relationships:

Physical and Mental Abuse

Some parents (typically alcoholics and addicts) may violently abuse their children. In contrast, others may verbally abuse them by criticizing, shouting at, or continuously putting them down, harming the child. Youngsters who have been abused as children may grow up to be abusive adults who mistreat their parents and children, creating a vicious cycle.

Poor Communication

It can be aggravating when there is little or no communication between the parent and the child. This is frequently caused by parents believing that their children do not listen to them and youngsters believing that their parents do not understand them. This viewpoint prevents the two from communicating, resulting in resentment, bitterness, and sadness.

Co-dependency

Some parent-child relationships are codependent, in which the child is expected to look after the parents, particularly if one of them is incapacitated or terminally sick. As a result, the youngster assumes responsibility for making the parent happy, resolving family conflicts, or even taking on household tasks. They may also prioritize their parents' needs over their own, resulting in a codependent mentality.

Mistrust

Parents have a hard time trusting their children if they make errors or behave badly regularly. So if parents want their children to regain their trust, they must offer them the opportunity to demonstrate their trustworthiness.

It is undeniable that Parenting is difficult. However, as a mature and responsible adult, it is your responsibility to establish a healthy and loving bond with your child that makes life easier for both of you.

Chapter 5: Warmth and Nurturance

In the previous chapter, we discussed positive and negative Parenting, the dos and don'ts of raising a happy child, and the relationship between a child and parent. In this chapter, we shall discuss parents' warmth and loving interaction. The goal is to provide structure and help your kids grow and become the best they can be.

<u>What is Parental Warmth?</u>

Parental warmth is a feeling that gives a child assurance that they are not just loved but also treated lovingly. It is critical and, of course, a necessary ingredient that requires conscious effort from all parents to make their children's lives better. For example, warmth could motivate the child, applying humor and creating empathy to caution the child to behave well and against making them feel worthless or damned. It could also mean physical gestures such as hugging the child closely to soothe them when hurt. This means that sometimes, your words and advice will suffice, and you may need to show them you care through deliberate actions.

Similarly, warmth can be a bit trickish, such that instead of struggling and wanting to compel a child to do your will, you could employ enthusiasm to appease them to do the right thing. Parents often unintentionally lash out, maybe due to fatigue, being overwhelmed, unhappy, taken for granted, maltreated, or even misunderstood. At this point, the warmth has been thrown out of the window. Warmth should not be seasonal; it should be expressed from time to time; as such, it usually finds its expression when your heart is peaceful as against when you are unsettled or in a bad state of mind. Essentially, irrespective of your thoughts or situation at any point in time, you need to exude warmth. You can work on your warmth towards your kids using a few tips. You may have to work on yourself at all times, especially on your emotions. The truth is, you can't give what you don't have, and as such if your emotional; life is balanced, you would have the intuition for nurturing and caring appropriately for your kids. Also, you could try out meditation practices to help you stay peaceful. You can also work on the relationship that is stripping off your peace. Finally, if you feel you are in a critical state, you might need help from a professional or a therapist. According to experts, warm, responsive, and supportive parenting behaviors are related to continuous improvement, positive change, and overall wellbeing from childhood into adulthood.

The Essence of Parental Warmth

The most important or influential individuals in everyone's lives are parents. It is only normal for a child to look up to his parents. Parental warmth cannot be overlooked as every parent's noteworthy essence. For a child, parental warmth is the feeling projected by their parents to make them believe that they are important and loved and can go to their parents irrespective of whatever situation they find themselves in. A child's level usually determines the kind of warmth you should exhibit as a parent. For example, at birth, a child requires the warmth of his mother to be able to survive. And while growing up, a child constantly requires motivation, humor, and empathy. The idea is usually to understand your child well enough to help them modify their behavior instead of an unrealistic approach of criticizing the child and making them feel less valued. While your children grow older, most times, you need to take positive actions rather than talking and trying to guide them with word of mouth. You could sit beside them and even wrap your hand around their shoulder, isn't that cool? Let's dive into why parental warmth is crucial in a child's life.

The child feels loved and important: the idea of being loved is so intriguing that it gives an individual a sense of existence. When a child doesn't get attention, it usually harms them mentally, academically, and socially. You would find out that some children often look lost while in class; they tend to seclude themselves from others, resulting from not being nurtured by their parents. Constantly reassuring a child of being loved positively impacts them until adulthood.

Helps in the self-expression of the child's potentials: Parents' constant affirmation of love makes it easier for their kids to explore their potential. Usually, the non-judgmental approach creates an environment for the kids to feel safe expressing their potential freely. Warmth makes these kids portray gifts you would naturally not know they have; thus, they can get better each day.

Helps a child to communicate their thoughts: Parental warmth gives children the free-hand to express their feelings, whether positive or negative. Teens or young adults whose parents are nurturing have the confidence to share their grief with their parents; it gives them a sense of relief that they would always listen and not criticize them.

Children who don't have nurturing parents tend to have flawed personalities. They don't trust people and are always perplexed that they might be abandoned. Thus, it is clear that parental warmth is essential in helping a child become a great adult and fosters the parent-children relationship.

Parenting with a Sense of Humor

Humor is necessary for relationships and emotional wellbeing. Humor counteracts negative moods like anxiety and depression and boosts positive emotions. Most Parents believe that being a comic or jokester as a form of nurturing style is a departure or distraction from the routine of Parenting. Contrary to that, humor is a more effective tool to take charge of certain situations. A parent can calm a child, encourage good behavior, and create a potentially parent-child solid bond with a sense of humor. Humor can be used to reduce tension in different areas of life, including Parenting, though most parents underestimate its power. Think about it. Have you tried your best to correct that child while you were angry? Did the anger bring about any change in the child's behavior? Well, the answer is No. Approaching a child with anger may only wedge your relationship, but a simple joke or humor could melt a child's heart. Your jokes do not encourage the child, but it's just a trickish style to calm your child and help them understand the right things to do. Now, jokes, laughter, or sarcasm can be made derogatory, but this is not good for a child and can severely damage your relationship.

On the contrary, you don't have to apply humor to critical situations that could expose your child to unnecessary risk or danger health-wise, in their academics, physically, or even socially. Such cases demand that you impose restrictions and call them to order. The principle of humor in Parenting is to, first of all, love your child irrespective of the immediate misstep. That way, you have the situation under control and reduce the child's feelings of regrets or remorse after doing things inappropriately.

Humor is capable of stirring an individual to become happy, and it is a social connection that has been proven to work with children to address missteps or misbehaviors. Interestingly, humor doesn't only help the child but also the parent, as it tends to reduce the parent's anger during a tense situation.

Let's say, for instance:

Your child dismantles your make-up box and breaks your expensive lipstick.

Your child takes your car to the mall after warning him against it, and your front mirror gets broken.

Your toddler, whom you just changed her dress, sat on the garden floor and managed to stain her dress.

Your teenager kids, whom you've warned against playing ball within the house, broke the living room window.

Your teenager, whom you thought to constantly wash her dirty dishes immediately after use, piled up all the dishes in the kitchen and started playing to keep consistent.

Honestly, not a single act is hilarious at the time of occurrence. You would need to control your anger and use a new approach. For example, you can coin a slang like "You gotta eat the cheese you spewed" and then make it an inside joke that you repeat whenever they misstep. Alternatively, you can funnily swing your hand or jump up and down without uttering a word. You kids would find it funny, but they would at the same time understand your message and stop what they are doing. You need to always consider the effect of misbehavior in your child's life before you angrily react. If you feel your child's behavior doesn't warrant an actual punishment, then you can try some of these funny approaches.

Create a comic scene: You could funnily drag your feet and quit talking to disapprove of their behavior at that moment. Although this appears funny to your kids, they understand that the signal put them to order.

Swoop in: When they create a mess, pretend to join them in the cleaning up to diffuse the situation.

Pretend to be emotional: You can pretend like you're crying or unhappy without saying a word to make them understand they were wrong.

Make jest of your action: Laugh over it together when you make a mistake.

Invent a tune: You could create a song or a funny sound constantly when your kids break the rules to put them in check.

Usually, when a child falters, they expect you to get angry and lash out, but when you handle the situation in a naturally funny way, they become flabbergasted. So, change the tempo and deflect your child's apprehension, as humor gives them the chance to reflect on their actions and have a rethink. Wouldn't you do anything to avoid creating a wedge between the relationship of you and your kids, right? So then, add a little humor every time.

Extrinsic Motivation

When a child is encouraged to do something because of outside (extrinsic forces), it is referred to as extrinsic motivation. Kids can be motivated to do something to receive a reward, prize, praise, or other benefits or discouraged from doing something due to the consequences. Therefore, motivation can either be positive or negative.

Examples of extrinsic motivation are:

- Winning a race to win a medal
- Doing all house chores to play with friends
- Doing all homework on time before watching TV
- The rewards, prizes, and benefits of extrinsic motivation signal that a child has done well to have achieved such a feat.

The problem with extrinsic motivation is that when you stop to motivate the child, he may have excellent performance as usual. People in general, especially kids, operate excellently well when they get validation from outside. However, as a child grows up, you may send the wrong signal if you continue to offer external rewards for good behavior. He would believe that people get rewards for good behavior, which is not valid. Life doesn't work that way, so it is expedient that you help your child build intrinsic motivation when necessary.

<u>Intrinsic Motivation</u>

When a kid behaves appropriately because he understands that it is rewarding to do so, it is referred to as intrinsic motivation. It is when a child does things without expecting a form of appraisal or appreciation. The child does it out of free will and is not be coerced to do so. A pressman says, "the intrinsic motivation is when things are done based on the reasons inside of a child; the child is motivated to learn or do something."

Examples of intrinsic motivation are:

- Playing table tennis because he likes and enjoys doing so.

- Flushing the toilet because they know not doing so could get subsequent users irritated.
- Doing their homework on time because they feel fulfilled afterward.
- Getting their chores done because they knew doing so would relieve other family members.

How Do You Help a Child Develop Motivation?

Developing a child's intrinsic motivation can be a challenging task. The right way to help a child stay motivated is to support the internal drivers with the appropriate external feedback. Then, when your child becomes fully internally motivated, you do not have to interrupt it with external commentaries to avoid losing sight of their internal drive.

Some of the tips for developing internal motivation in kids are:

Guide them to make good choices on achievable goals and challenge them from time to time.

Help your kids identify the specific things they can accomplish and help them push away every barrier and obstacle.

Always check your kids to ensure that they behave appropriately and guide them to check themselves.

Don't spoil them unnecessarily with rewards; however, you can do that a few times to motivate them to do things they find a bit complicated.

Praise them for striving through the long process of achieving their set goals and not forgetting the end goal.

You need always be their role model, so be conscious of your behavior. If you teach them what you fail to act, they will never be motivated to follow your words.

Motivating Your Children

A parent's constant support and encouragement are needed to keep a child motivated. Children usually look up to their parent's direction as they consider them their biggest fan and cheerleader. There are several ways to motivate your child; let's dive into them.

Celebrate accomplishments: Do not overlook it when a child does well accomplishing their goal. Instead, celebrate it as that will encourage them to do more.

Teach them to compete healthily: tell them that they can come first in a race or emerge the best student in their class. It gives them a sense of strength that nothing is impossible to achieve.

Please help them realize their passion: Spend time with your children to help them discover what they are passionate about. Then, please help them become better by encouraging them and even seeking information to enlighten them appropriately.

Stay positive: You can't motivate your children if you don't garner enough motivation yourself. So always put up a positive outlook on things and be confident while having no doubts whatsoever.

Have Meaningful Conversations: Always have a one-on-one talk with your kids. Children are naturally curious; they want to ask questions and understand different subjects. Therefore, inviting them for a talk may appeal to their intellect. Talk to your kids, answer their questions, and get feedback.

Act as a role model: You can't always have rancor with your spouse every time and expect them not to fight when they get to school or even have disagreements with their siblings. Whatever you want your child to do, Act it! You want them to use the words like 'thank you' and 'please'; use them yourself. Please don't say what you do not mean in the presence of your children, as they take you by your words.

Embrace their imperfections: Even adults are not perfect, let alone kids. However, you are their parents and need to understand their strengths and weaknesses. For example, if you find out your child doesn't like a chore, you can use creativity to make her find it appealing.

Key Takeaway

As parents, your goal is to get to know your child well enough, figure out his strengths and weaknesses and help influence him to do something he would ordinarily not do with his effort. In addition, you should strengthen your child's skills in identifying what is important to him and motivate them to figure out who they are.

Chapter 6: Of Boundaries and Limits

A very challenging task in Parenting is saying "No" to your child. When a child starts to understand and speak languages, most parents feel like every word they speak is either "No" or "Stop." That's because almost everything they say to the child begins with "No" or "Stop." For instance, they say "Stop doing that," or "No, I won't give you," or "Not on the bed," or other sentences related to that. Although it can be frustrating and tiring to say "No," you should understand that it is a critical part of Parenting. Saying "No" to your kids is one of the best things to help a child, especially when they are very young.

When you say "No" to your children, you teach them boundaries. Children must learn boundaries from home because that's the first place to learn how to abide by several rules (written or unwritten) in society. When a child is not exposed to boundaries at home, such a child will find it difficult to abide by rules in school. Likewise, if they cannot follow the rules in school, they will find it difficult to abide by rules that guide society at large.

For successful Parenting, the important thing about setting boundaries is not only about saying "No." How you say "No" is also very important. In this chapter, we will navigate how to set boundaries successfully.

<u>When Boundaries are Needed</u>

Children are normally curious; they want to know everything. For example, once a child starts crawling and walking, they want to explore their environment; they want to know places in the house by themselves. That is why you see that they move around to places you never expected at any opportunity they get. This curious attitude is a sign of potential danger, and that's why you need to set boundaries. You need to make simple rules that guide them on what to do and what not to do. As a child continues to grow, they need to set rules on interacting with people and objects. The rules help keep them safe from dangers and enhance their behavior around others. For instance, you can tell your one-year toddler to be gentle with her friend or put her shoe on the shoe rack.

There is no age limit in setting boundaries for kids; it could start as young as when breastfeed until they grow into an adult. Setting boundaries for your sucking child may be as simple as bathing them even if they cry during the process. The child is indirectly learning that his cry won't stop you from bathing him. The mistake most parents make is thinking a child is too small to learn how to follow the rules. Irrespective of a child's age, they learn. It may not be about telling them dos and don'ts, but your reaction to some situations will make them know your stand on particular issues. Most parents who don't set boundaries for their children at a younger age find it difficult to do so when they become teenagers. It's better to start teaching your children whatever you want them to know as early as possible.

You might not have been taking boundaries seriously before. Still, when any of the following things I will mention below starts to happen, it is a clear indication that you need to level up on your boundary-setting game.

- Your 12-year-old child barges into your room and doesn't regard your privacy.
- Your 9-year-old child interrupts your discussion with other people without seeking permission.

- Your teenager is dictating how to live your life after a divorce.
- Your kid wants you to do something and then throw tantrums if you do otherwise.

The list is endless, but once your child exhibits any of these behaviors, it is high time you start setting boundaries.

Setting boundaries should not be mistaken for being authoritative. Rules are good for children because it gives them a sense of security. Setting boundaries allows your children to differentiate between what is acceptable and not acceptable. When boundaries are not set for children, they become anxious and lost because they have too much freedom to do whatever they like.

The Essence of Parental Boundaries

Setting boundaries for kids can be difficult for various reasons. Sometimes, you may feel guilty for saying "No," or you try to prevent your child from throwing tantrums when you set some limits. No matter how difficult setting boundaries may be for you, you must understand that it is important for the children. Setting boundaries is not just said for saying sake; it is important to teach a child good behavior and gives them the privilege to enhance some of their skills. As we proceed, I will explain some of the importance of setting boundaries for kids and open your eyes to why you should not take it for granted.

Boundaries Help Kids to be Self-Disciplined

Boundaries help to develop the self-discipline skills of a child. For instance, when you ask your kid to switch off the TV and do his homework, you teach that child to be self-disciplined.

Although the show she is watching on TV is entertaining, you teach her that her academics are more important. The aim is to let your children be responsible for schoolwork, house chores, and other important things without reminders.

By setting boundaries, you are helping your children to learn how to be disciplined no matter how enjoyable other stuff is. For example, you can set a timer for ten minutes and ask your children to beat the timer. You can tell your kids that they can only play games after completing their homework. Let your child show that he is responsible for your set boundaries. If they don't cross the boundaries, you know they are becoming more responsible and can trust them with other things.

Boundaries Help Your Children to be Safe

Boundaries teach your children how to be safe in the environment. For example, when allowing your kids to play outside, you can set boundaries of where and where not to go. Boundaries also help your kids to be safe when they start using gadgets. For example, you can limit the amount of time on the internet. That will help them not waste their time online when they grow into adults. The boundaries you set for kids can increase as they continue to grow.

Boundaries Help to Keep Children Healthy

Naturally, children are impulsive, and they love pleasure, and that is why you need to teach them how to stay healthy. You should set boundaries on what and when your children eat. If you allow your kids to have access to everything they crave, you might be pushing them to an early grave because bad eating habits will lead to bad health. Setting boundaries means saying, "No, you can't eat cookies today," or "No, you can't eat late in the night.," and many others.

You should set boundaries regarding electronics and gadgets. Children don't mind watching TV or video games all day long, but it can diminish their cognitive development. They need to have limits on when to watch their shows. Set boundaries with their sleep time, hygiene, screen time, and other practices to enhance healthy living.

Boundaries Help Children to Cope with Uncomfortable Emotions

Sometimes, parents don't set boundaries because they don't want their children to feel sad or angry. Meanwhile, learning to cope with uncomfortable emotions is an important skill everyone should have, including kids. For example, your child may be sad because you didn't allow her to eat a cookie, but that is not enough reason to change your words. Setting boundaries allows your children to cope with emotions and find healthy ways to deal with them.

Boundaries will help your children to learn how to control their emotions. Boundaries will help them learn how to deal with anger, sadness, frustration, or boredom. Instead of calming your children down or cheering them up, let them know the reason why you have chosen to restrict those things from them. By doing that, they will know the reasons for your actions and discover ways to get out of such emotions. Children who know how to control their emotions are better prepared for adulthood.

Boundaries Show Your Children That You Care

Most times, children cross boundaries to see your reaction. For example, a child may decide to jump on the chair after being warned to stop or hit a younger sibling in your presence. Sometimes, these children may want to test their leadership skills. Children who live without boundaries experience anxiety.

Children are not designed to be in charge. You need to let your children know that you are in charge and trust you to help them do the right thing. By giving a negative consequence for crossing a boundary, you show your children that you are in control. Negative consequences should not be mistaken for child abuse or maltreating of a child. It could be as simple as not allowing her to watch TV.

Setting boundaries also shows that you love your children and are willing to do anything to ensure that they live well. For example, when you tell your child, "I love you, and that's why I am not going to allow you to eat another cookie," he may be offended for a while. But it indicates that you are ready to give it whatever it takes for your children to live the best lives.

<u>Know Where to Draw the Limit</u>

Many unnecessarily punish children in the name of setting boundaries. You should know that your kids are kids and can never be perfect. Sometimes, parents set boundaries, and they wonder why they are ineffective. As I said earlier, setting boundaries is not as important as how you set them. We will discuss how to set boundaries that effectively raise children below.

Give Simple and Direct Instructions

When giving your kids instructions, kindly make it simple to understand. Give them instructions that are not ambiguous and will be easy for them to follow. Your instructions should be direct and close-ended. For instance, let us look at two statements below.

Statement 1: "Why not finish your assignment before watching TV?"

Statement 2: "Please, finish your assignment before watching TV."

Looking at the two statements, you observe that statement 2 is more direct and close-ended than statement 1. That is because statement 1 asks for the child's opinion, but statement two tells your child what she must do before watching TV. As a result, your child will quickly understand what you are saying and adhere to your instructions.

Consistency

When you are consistent with the set boundaries, your children become more familiar with them. When you constantly force rules in the house, there will be discipline and structure, which are important factors for effective Parenting. Children find it easier to keep to rules when you constantly impose on them. Also, being consistent with boundaries shows that you are serious about them, which teaches them that they are responsible for their actions. Finally, being firm with your boundaries will make them reconsider before crossing any boundary.

Give Appropriate Body Language

We must have all heard that body language contributes to communicating a message. That is also relevant when setting boundaries for children. When teaching a child, make the appropriate eye contact, voice, and facial expression to suit the message. For example, don't expect to discipline a child smiling or laughing. On the other hand, you wouldn't be convinced if someone tries to discipline you while laughing. As long as your body language corresponds to what you say, your child will know that you mean what you say. Keeping the appropriate body language will help them to stay within boundaries.

Be Firm with Your Decisions and Consequences

Normally, our children ought not to be upset with us. However, it's normal for your child to be mad at you when setting boundaries. They have to learn about appropriate and inappropriate behavior no matter the circumstance. Don't compromise on your decisions because your children feel bad about it. Children may not love it when you set boundaries, but you have to because they need it. You may be tempted to withdraw the consequences for crossing a boundary, but I want you to know that empty threats will not solve the problem either. Empty threats may make your children happy with you for a moment, but you are indirectly telling them that you do not take such boundaries seriously. Your children may go ahead to cross that and many other boundaries in the future because they feel that you cannot do anything.

Acknowledge when they stick to the set boundaries.

Acknowledging your children shows them that you care about them even after doing something wrong. Acknowledge your children when they do things right; praise them and appreciate their efforts. Children love to be praised for doing something, especially when it's coming from their parents. When you acknowledge your children for sticking to a boundary, they will be motivated to continue so they can have that good feeling again. Appreciation and acknowledgment are great ways to make children stick to boundaries.

Set Reasonable Boundaries

In setting boundaries, don't set awkward and unreasonable boundaries. You need to understand what can be done by a child at a particular age. Don't expect the same things from a three-year-old child and a ten-year-old child. When you recognize that some boundaries are unnecessary, it will help you not have high expectations and save you from unnecessary stress.

Don't Allow Your Kids to Control Your Home

In other words, don't spoil your kids. Children develop a high level of authority when given much control and power in the house. When your kids are in charge, the boundaries you set begin to get blurred. They might develop boldness to go against your boundaries and do what you tell them. When children are given too much control, they struggle and have serious conflicts with their parents when they grow older. If you don't curb your children from when they are young, you will find it difficult to set boundaries when they become teenagers, as teens tend to seek independence.

In conclusion, setting boundaries is important in raising a responsible child. Boundaries help kids to differentiate between acceptable and unacceptable behaviors. Boundary setting is beneficial for kids because it helps them stay healthy, safe, responsible, and emotionally balanced. To make boundary setting effective, you need to be consistent. You also have to set reasonable boundaries so that your expectations will not be cut short. In setting boundaries, let your children know the reason behind such boundaries, as this will help them to be able to stick to them.

Key Takeaway

- Children must learn boundaries from home.
- Setting boundaries should not be mistaken for being authoritative.
- Boundaries help to develop the self-discipline skills of a child.

- By setting boundaries, you allow your children to cope with emotions.
- Consistency is vital when setting boundaries.

Chapter 7: Balancing Parenting, Work and Life

The previous chapter has opened your eyes to where to draw a line in relating with your child; the next thing is to strike a balance between work and parenting. Parenting a child can be pretty stressful due to specific responsibilities and changes in one's life. These changes and responsibilities arise to satisfy some needs in the family and the child's life. To meet these needs, parents can find themselves succumbing to stress, affecting their relationships. These stress simulators could be from overworking, correcting a child and others. Apart from the stress, when your work takes most of your life, you would have little or no time to relate with your child(ren). Therefore, parents need to strike a balance between work and healthy parenting. This chapter provides you with insights on creating a balance between your work and parenting. Follow me through the tips I am about to share.

<u>Coping with Stress</u>

It is easy to snap at another person when you are agitated because of your uneasiness while under pressure. However, it would be best to learn to control your reactions when relating with people in this state. If you don't manage your stress level very well, you will likely ruin your relationship. As a parent, you have to master yourself rather than let stress manipulate you. In my early days of employment, I had a lot of deadlines to meet, and I still had to run some things around the house. Things got pretty tight for me because I had little time to rest at home. As a result, I usually get cranky at the slightest mistake other family members make. It almost caused a rift between my family and me but, I'm glad I got over it quickly, thanks to loving corrections from my family.

Now that you've seen a side of my story, I'm sure you would relate to it so, how can you cope with stress;

Ask for Help

You are not the first working parent, and you won't be the last so, why not ask other experienced parents how they managed themselves. Some parents might be experienced in handling stress but not successful in the course, so look out for the outstanding ones. Your elderly/young neighbors or parents could be an option, so help yourself by contacting them. When things get overwhelming, you can ask your partner to assist around the house. As a single parent, you can consider reaching out to your close relatives for some help around the house, or you could converse with your employer about work appointments that will benefit you and your family. However, if you can't control it with this step or you still feel more irritated than necessary, you can seek the aid of a psychiatrist or psychologist.

Go Easy on Yourself

Avoid overworking yourself; you are not a robot so, take on a task that you can cope with. Understand your work and find easy ways to navigate through. When you do this, your burden will be reduced. Hence, you won't have to carry your work home. Take a deep breath and do things that energize you, like playing games, watching movies or singing. You can tune in to your favorite subject. In addition to this, try to chat with your kids for a few minutes. Communicating with your kids can improve your relationship, which relaxes your mind.

Be Optimistic

Managing your family and working are two different things, but if you don't see the positive side, then these two things could cause you to crash. Rather than focus on the problems in the house or how complex your child is, you should look at all the good things circulating the two. If your child is having a hard time in school and you've done your best to help him perform well, you can try other things like making them feel good about themselves. You can outline specific unique traits they are oblivious. For instance, there was a time my friend's daughter was bad at science, and her father told her to study harder. To avoid disappointing her parents, she did all she could, but she would often get confused and frustrated in class regardless of any explanation given by the teacher. It got worse that she started feeling inferior, and she took it upon herself to bully those doing well in her class. Her parents were so ignorant of what was going on due to their work before her homeroom teacher called for their attention. At first, her father was mad at her, but he later opened her eyes to see her resilience (she has always been resilient from infancy) and how bullying others won't make her any better. "You should have seen the smile she wore"; my friend told me. Together, we worked out the root of the difficulty in the subject. Retorted, my friend as we are discussing our experiences as parents.

Apart from work stress, other things can also trigger your stress level in parenting. These triggers include; bullying reports from your child, underweight or overweight, poor grades at school. You should note that these can make you feel agitated to the point of taking strong measures in and outside the house.

Create a Routine

How organized are you? Do you know that it can affect your productivity and relationship if you don't coordinate yourself and your activities? Therefore, you need to get organized because you can only be in complete control of your life and activities when this is cultivated. You can achieve this by creating a routine. It has to do with taking note of all engagement and activities. For instance, when you get to work, you can go through all the assigned tasks and set them in order of importance and urgency. Doing this will give you a clear mind on performing such tasks. It will also increase your productivity, so you will be home on time to attend to your family. In addition, you can arrange your chores and even fix a day for tedious ones.

Every weekend, I make sure I clean every part of the house. Unlike other people, I don't overwhelm myself with cleaning during the week. I just created an easy way by apportioning some tasks to some days. I have been enjoying this routine for a while now, so you can create one and see the changes. You can create a routine by observing the following tips.

Identify what you want- It is essential you know what you plan on achieving before creating any routine. Being aware of your wants keeps you focused and productive in the long run. Then, just like my example, you can create a routine that will make your chores enjoyable and less cumbersome.

Set a target- It is not enough to plan; you can start working with little chores or tasks at work and home. If you think you are not spending enough time with your kids, come up with a time to have a chit-chat with them. Start with thirty minutes if your schedule is tight.

Embrace Consistency- It's not a crime to get tired or try to rush things when it looks convenient. However, it will benefit you if you are consistent with your plans. Follow through no matter how busy you are, and gradually, you will develop a habit out of it.

Enjoy the process- Don't go too hard on your plans. Take some moments to bask in the plan. You can switch on your radio or music stereo to accompany you as you work. It's not a crime to crack some jokes with your family as you work; try to make each moment as memorable as possible.

Now that you know how to navigate those demanding tasks, the next thing is to create a family-friendly routine. The previous section was all about you, so how do you carry the other members along; note that this routine has to be planned, anticipated and regular (consistency). The effect of this is to help the family bond, create a good family time, and instill a sense of duty in each family member.

Routines to Make

Initiate a chat time- your children could belong to talk to you, but if you are constantly consumed with work, be it outside or inside the home, you will create an immeasurable distance between yourselves. You don't want to be estranged from your children. You can set the pace by discussing how your day went at work, what you saw on the news, and get their opinion about things around the neighborhood. They will get connected with you and express themselves without being forced as you do this.

Story session- If you have children who love stories, you can read bedtime stories and even share your funny experiences with them. This goal is to make them feel loved even if they are occupied with other things. When you start this, you will find that you will start looking forward to moments like that.

Share Chores- Let each family member know what is expected of them around the house. It helps in coordinating things around the home and helps them work better as a team.

Exercise- It is a way of bonding with your body and children. Try working out in the morning or take an evening stroll with your child or children.

Creating a routine helps the family through the daily tasks efficiently and effectively, creating time for other things.

Designating Approved Activities

Since you are now aware of how routine creation can help in improving your parenting duties even when you are working. You need to focus on the type of activities you approve for your child. These activities go a long way in building them even in your absence. However, you need to know the thin line between controlling your children through these activities and guiding them. Consider any approved activities by weighing their effects on your child's life. I'm sure you don't want to factor any regret into their life. You need to know your child before designating any activities before even approving them. Don't force anything on them; if it benefits them, talk them calmly into it. Therefore, there are factors to consider when choosing these activities.

Age

It would help if you considered your child's age before settling for any activity. You can't expect a four-year-old child to do what a 12-year-old would do. Sometimes, interest comes with age, so you shouldn't rush your kid to do anything.

Convenience

Children work best when they are not pressured. Anything you decide for your child shouldn't clash with their fun time; it turns them off, and they might likely react with a strong aversion to it.

Instead, let them take on tasks, assignments and chores with a relaxed mind- it makes things enjoyable that way.

Type of Activity

Here, you still have to consider your child's personality and interests to achieve a better result. For example, you can sign your child up for singing lessons if they are interested in it. You can also pick on activities that will heighten your child's curiosity- Children are inquisitive, so you can boost this by getting a spectacular object of interest for them. In addition, if your child pursues what is harmful to him or against the family's values, you can talk him out of it. They need to do what makes them and every other family member happy. Finally, it would be best to consider such activities' impact on your child's life. Don't settle for the fun only; ask yourself these questions; does it make them assertive? Does it foster team spirit in them? Can they learn perseverance from this? And many other life polishing questions.

Activities To Designate for Your Child

After answering those questions and considering the age and convenience, you can choose activities that will benefit them in the long run. These activities are divided into two.

Outdoor Activities

Activities under this category are meant to be done outside the confines of the wall house. Most of them are sporting activities, although there are some sports they can do within the house walls. They are usually done under the supervision of an experienced and elder figure. You can either coordinate them or supervise them. Such activities include; visiting the park, going on a picnic, climbing a tree, jumping on a trampoline, drawing, watching the stars, playing tennis, visiting the beach, building a snowman (during winter), cycling and lots more.

Indoor Activities

Activities like these are performed IN-doors. They help your child develop a sense of warmth towards others and themselves because they are done under the cozy allure of a place that is mainly in the home. It also paves the way for child creativity because they will do things for fun without going outside. Such activities include; making a meal, solving puzzles, fixing some broken items, playing video games, doing dance and singing competitions, reading books, rearranging the house, styling each other's hair, decorating the house, doing some house or canvas painting and many more things to explore.

You can also introduce your child to meditation exercises.

Revisit Your Schedule

Before you initiate any activities for your kids, you need to check your schedule. Try to remove insignificant things and focus on building your relationship with your child. For instance, you can remove a chit-chat meeting you have with your colleagues after work to pick up your child or children from school. In addition, before you choose any activity, confirm your presence with them by canceling any hindrance.

In conclusion, being a parent and working can trigger some adverse reactions from you, and it can even mar your relationship with your child, but you can manage the two if you are determined. First, you have to identify the root of your stress to cope with it, and this is achievable by asking for help, going easy on yourself and facing problems with an optimistic approach. You can afterward create a routine to coordinate all your activities. Such a routine must be planned and regular and designed to benefit and involve every member of your family. A routine makes work and domestic life worthwhile for you. Afterward, you can designate approved activities for your children. These activities are stimulants that will direct your child and instill some unique values in his life. You can finally revisit your schedule to align the previous points into shape.

Chapter 8: Building Effective Communication

In the previous chapter, we focused on how you can achieve a work-parenting balance such that we would be able to overcome stress, create a routine, designate approved activities, and revisit schedules. Parenting requires a lot of preparation and communicating effectively with kids is one of the crucial keys to knowing these children and building a positive relationship with them. Research has shown that it is pretty easy for adults to keep in touch with children through conversation and attention. Parents who have good communication with their kids talk with them regularly about different subjects, including alcohol, drugs etc. and not just when there is conflict. Depending on your child's age, there are different styles of communicating with children. For instance, about a few years back, my colleague dressed her toddler up in very decent and beautiful outfit, and they were up for the Sunday service in the church. She could feel all the excitement on her daughter's face as she seemed to like bright colors.

When they stepped out of the door, she remembered she didn't take the snacks she had bought for her. She quickly rushed in to pick it up in the living room, and by the time she got outside, she saw her daughter sitting down on the dusty balcony. It wasn't even funny! Now, some parents will shout at their kids at that time to make them realize they misstepped. But, do you know what she did? She smiled at her daughter, took her inside the house, removed the dress and showed the little girl how dirty it was. Then, she dressed her up in another beautiful bright-colored dress. It's simple! She passed her information to the young girl without uttering a word. In a case where a teenager misbehaves, you could sit them down and guide them to doing the right thing. Generally speaking, nothing beats the idea of having a smooth relationship with your kids via good communication.

Understanding Your Child's Love Language

Humans have basic emotional needs, and children are no exception. Your kids have tons of emotional needs that you must meet if you want them to grow as emotionally stable individuals. Children need love and affection, and they want to have that sense of feeling that they belong. According to Gary Chapman, "every child has an emotional tank that yearns to be filled with love. "As such, when you see a child misbehaving repeatedly, it is a result of the cravings of their empty love tank. Every child has a love language. If you want to give and receive love in the most effective way possible, you must learn to speak the correct language. What makes your child feel loved? Let's briefly see the five types of love languages for children.

Physical Contact

You don't need a special occasion or excuse to make physical contact; as such, it is the most uncomplicated love language to use for your children. Examples of physical touch are hugs, kisses, a pat on the head or even a gentle touch at the back. As parents, you have an endless opportunity to transfer love to the heart of your kids through constant touch. You could try out the following if you feel your child's love language is touch:

- Hug and kiss your child before they leave home for school and at night when tucking them into bed.

- Cuddle your child on the sofa while watching a movie.

- Hold your child's hand as you walk.

- Brush your boy's hair and stroke your girl's hair when you are having deep conversations.

- You can squeeze your child's shoulder gently as you walk past.

- Place them on your lap for younger children and tell them beautiful stories or even watch their favorite cartoon with them.

Affirmative Words: Words are powerful and capable of lifting up or pulling down. Children take note of everything we say and whatever we say to them has a significant effect on their life, whether positive or negative. For your child, if his love language is words of affirmation, then you need to use words of appreciation or verbal compliments as a communicator of love to help affirm and reaffirm your children's self-worth. You could try out the following if you feel your child's love language is words of affirmation:

- Remind them repeatedly that you love them and will never stop doing so.

- Compliment them when they do well.

- Let them overhear you saying good things about them to someone.

- For teenagers, you could send them messages reminding them that they mean a lot to you.

- Give them a sweet pet name that you only use for them and no other person.

Attention: Some children want you to give them full attention. This love language is a bit tasking, unlike words of affirmation and physical contact. Dedicating quality time for someone is not easy; therefore, you need to reschedule your activities and arrange your time judiciously to incorporate this. For every opportunity you have with your child, you need to make sure that you do things together and know each other well enough. You could try out the following if you feel your child's love language is attention:

- Make constant eye contact with your child when you are having a conversation.

- Before tucking your child into bed, please spend some time with them; you could even read them interesting stories or make them tell you about their day.

- Add humor to your gestures, play and laugh together

- Spend time to play their favorite game or hobby with them

- Take them to special places or events and spend time together

- Spend time to assist them with their homework

Giving Gifts: Gifts are not payments for services rendered. They are given as an expression of love for an individual, and the giver gives freely without requesting anything in return. If your child's love language is giving gifts, then you'd need to use a combination of gifts, words of affirmation and physical touch to make that child feel loved. Gifts are not necessarily expensive things and have little to do with size, and it's just a natural expression of love. If you send your child to wash the dirty dishes and then give her a gift afterward, this is merely a payment for services and not a true gift. As parents, you need to know that you can't substitute one love language for another. You could try out the following if you feel your child's love language is gifting:

- You can hide a gift that interests your child in his lunchbox

- Give them beautiful flowers after a walk

- When your child is not at home, mail a small package for them

- Get your child a unique gift like jewelry, clothes, shoes etc. with their name customized on it

Acts of Service: Loving Service is a desire that comes naturally from within to give energy to others without being motivated to do so. Parents perform different acts of service for their kids, from doing their laundry to cleaning the dirty dishes to preparing them for school. All the tasks put together can be so vast and time-consuming to the point that some parents would begin to feel as though they are enslaved. The goal of acts of service to children is to show them love and build up the capacity in them to be able to love others. Even though you serve them to show them, love, you also teach them to serve themselves and other people.

You could try out the following if you feel your child's love language is an act of service:

- Help your child with their homework

- Assist your child in fixing his toy batteries when it breaks

- Make sure to give them food at the right time

- For you teenager, you could fill up the gas in their car

- Assist your child when he is practicing for his favorite sports in school

To discover and learn your child's primary love language, you need to be patient and devote your time to that child. By the time you understand their needs, it will help you bond closely with them in a way you never thought possible.

Initiate the Talk with Your Child

As parents, you can bring meaning into your daily conversations with your children. You can always initiate a conversation to open a new line of communication. The idea behind initiating conversations is to bond with your children and be attentive to their feelings and daily experiences. The state of your child at a particular time should determine how you choose to initiate a conversation. For instance, you could ask a sincere question with a soft tone, a positive question in an enthusiastic manner and a silly question in a funny voice as this can be the most constructive and appropriate way to get to know your concerns in-depth and also have an understanding of the child's state of mind. To start a conversation with your child, you may consider the following guidelines.

Choose the right time and place: Find an appropriate venue and a time where there would be no external interference to disrupt your chat. It would help if you made your child feel very comfortable and open for the talk, and you don't have to turn it into a 'special talk' moment.

Prepare to make the conversation flow: You need to make the conversation clear and smooth. It would be a total waste of time if your child couldn't hold on to any significant point at the end of your conversation. Instead, introduce the subject by citing a typical example or going straight to the point.

Let them know why you are bothered: As parents, you need to explain to your child the reasons why you are troubled and wish to talk to them. Otherwise, your child might feel that you are troubled for no reason. When you help your child understand your worries, they will become more receptive to changing and turning a new leaf.

Allow them to express themself: A chat is balanced only when it is interactive between the two parties. Sometimes you might be tempted to do all the talking alone, but you shouldn't do so. Instead, ask them positive questions to uplift them and give them time to respond to them. Similarly, listen to them more than you talk; this helps you have a broad view of their perspective regarding the subject and guide them accordingly.

Show them love and support: Irrespective of how difficult the conversation appears, it is crucial to show them that you care about them and that nothing can ever displace your love for them.

How You Can Encourage Family Discussion

Family discussions encourage members of the family to learn more about each other. In other words, conversations are crucial to family learning as this creates an avenue to having a deep understanding of each other. To have open communication amongst members of your family, we would give you tips that help this happen.

Hold regular meetings: Set a regular time to hold meetings and encourage each family member to stay committed and keep it as a priority. You can make the meeting as brief as possible but very interactive.

Alternate meeting responsibilities between members: Most families stay united because everyone is treated equally; thereby, rotating responsibilities between family members encourage everyone to participate in the program. An adult should take the leadership role of coordinating every family member and making sure everyone's point of view is heard.

Talk on one subject per time and proffer solutions: Talk on a specific topic that affects the family generally. Usually, there are so many things to be discussed, but you have to attend to the most pressing subjects at a go. Then, point at possible solutions and resolve issues accordingly.

If there's an argument, call for a break: You can call for a 15minutes break or more if your discussions become too hot to handle before meeting again.

End conversations on a funny note that reaffirms family members: initiate activities that every family member enjoys, such as games, movies, or the family's local dish.

Leverage the Power of Listening

Active listening is an effective way to enhance the communication between you and your child. It assures the child that you are interested in what they say. There are several ways to practice active listening, and we'd share them below.

Pay rapt attention to your child.

- Look into their eyes throughout the conversation.
- Stop whatever you are doing to concentrate on them
- Stoop low to their level
- Repeat what the child is saying to be sure you understand them

You might have had a bad day or been tired and not made a reservation to listen to your kids. But, you need to know that you have to take your child seriously whenever they have anything. Otherwise, they may end up taking the wrong steps and fall into problems due to negligence on your part. Similarly, listening to your kids gives them the willingness to talk to you about whatever bothers them even when they grow into adulthood.

Use a Word of Caution

There are ways to help a child yield to positive discipline. As parents, this job requires patience and time to give a child adequate warning and change from their bad behaviors; you need to do the following.

Help them understand: Teach your kids to know right from wrong using soothing words and actions.

Set rules and consequences: There's a saying that where there's no law, there's no sin. Thus, make them know the rules and consequences for going against it. It would help if you remembered that you have to be flexible too so as not to do any damage to them.

Listen to them: Listening to your child is very important as this is the only tool you can use to understand them and guide them appropriately. Pay attention to misbehaviors that have patterns, reinforce good character and discourage bad behaviors.

Let them experience natural consequences: You don't need to set stringent rules for everything as it is not something wrong and can cause them no harm. As such, let them understand natural consequences using their intuition. For example, if your child flings his toys to the wall, they will likely get damaged, and he would not be able to use them again. Soon, she'd learn that it is terrible to be destructive and change his actions positively.

Find out why they misstepped and redirect their actions: Sometimes, your kid might not be in the right state of mind or bored, thereby acting up. Find out what they want and help them get out of their troubles.

Become a Good Body Language User

There are several ways to communicate with your child, asides from using word of mouth. Using good body language as parents helps build up your kids' social skills. You could communicate using facial expressions and tone of voice and help them understand personal space. Kids usually don't understand body language, so you need to teach them. Do the following to help your child understand good body language.

Make sure your movement aligns with the message: make the child understand how different body movements can convey different messages and emotions.

Spot important Clues: Help your child point out examples both in real life and probably on TV to indicate and interpret how a person is feeling

Act it for them: You can act out emotions via body language to teach your children what each language means. For example, try illustrating emotions like happiness, anger, tiredness, being fed up etc.

<u>Handling Serious and Important Discussion</u>

One of the most challenging jobs about parenting is talking to your kids about complex subjects. But in this age of advanced technology, you have to discuss serious issues before they get exposed to other information on the internet. Of course, the way you handle discussions depends on the child's age. For kids between ages 2-6, you may need to do all you can to limit their exposure to inappropriate subjects, find out what they know, simplify the subject, and assure them that you're in charge. For ages 7-12, find out what they know, create a safe space for discussion, and address their curiosity. For teens, encourage an open dialogue, ask them questions to know their minds, share your values and proffer solutions to whatever is getting them worried.

Key Takeaway

Keep in mind that there are several things you can do to ensure effective communication between you and your children. First, remember that learning to interact with them is the only way to build the parent-child bond.

Chapter 9: Building the Emotions

Being a parent is genuinely an intensely emotional experience. Cuddling, playing, laughing, exploring, and delighting in your child's daily growth and discoveries is pure pleasure. Still, it's not without the difficult moments —moments of stress, anger, frustration, and resentment—from a crying baby who needs to be calmed, from a toddler's completely unreasonable demands, or an older child's aggressive behavior toward a new baby. These experiences elicit strong emotions that can be difficult to manage. However, it is essential to recognize and manage these emotions because how you react in these situations determines your child's development. Your reaction influences his ability to learn good coping skills and future behavior. Take, for example, a 2-year-old who is in tears because he can't cope with the fact that you gave him his cereal in the blue bowl rather than his favorite red bowl (as ridiculous as that may seem—such is life with a toddler). Reacting with anger and frustration is more likely to aggravate the child's distress than help him calm down and cope. Therefore, one of the most important ways to reduce your own— and your child's—distress is to learn to manage your reactions. It also teaches children how to manage their own emotions, which helps them perform better in school and develop friendships and other relationships as they grow.

Managing intense, negative emotions is undoubtedly easier said than done. But the effort is worthwhile because the payoff is enormous for both you and your child. So here are some guiding principles and strategies to consider:

Pay Attention to Your Emotions

Feelings are neither correct nor incorrect. What you do with your feelings can either help or hurt you. What's most important is that you pay attention to and own your emotions so that you can make a deliberate decision about how to respond rather than a knee-jerk reaction.

Examine Your Child's Behavior in the Context of Their Development and Temperament

Appropriate expectations are essential because the meaning you assign to your child's behavior influences how you manage your own emotions and reactions to the behavior at hand. For example, if you perceive the behavior as manipulative or intentionally hurtful (i.e., biting, hitting), you are more likely to react in ways that escalate rather than calm your child. And intense, angry reactions rarely result in the teaching of good coping skills. On the other hand, if you see these behaviors in the context of normal development, you can approach your child with empathy, increasing the likelihood that you will respond calmly and effectively.

Helping Your Children Grow Emotionally

Parenting is a demanding and ever-changing job; it goes without saying. As a parent, your role in their child's emotional development is one of the most important. The children that grow up to be emotionally aware adults are heavily influenced by their parents' stability and loving responses. Emotional development is complex; its architecture is built over time and requires a myriad of experiences and interactions. As parents, our job is to help our children understand their constantly changing emotions. They must identify what emotion they are experiencing, express different emotions in healthy ways, and regulate their emotions to respect others. Emotion regulation is essential for managing experiences and developing social-emotional intelligence.

Be Mindful of Their Emotions

Parenting is stressful and can feel never-ending. It's not always like running a marathon — it's more like running until you die. So, when things finally calm down, there's a natural tendency to look around and think, "Nothing is currently on fire." "All right, life is good." Emotions usually come before outbursts. As a result, recognizing the child's emotions early on — rather than just the resulting bad behavior — is critical.

Label Your Child's Feelings

Children must learn to recognize their emotions. You can assist your child by naming her emotions (at least the ones you suspect she is feeling). For example, when your child is upset because they lost a game at school, you can say, "It seems that you are outraged right now." Am I right?" If they appear sad, you could ask, "Are you disappointed that we aren't going to see Grandma and Grandpa today?" Emotional words like "angry," "upset," "shy," and "painful" can all contribute to a vocabulary for expressing feelings. Remember to include words for positive emotions such as "joy," "excited," "thrilled," and "hopeful."

Show Empathy

When your child is upset, it can be tempting to minimize how they're feeling, especially if their emotions come off a bit dramatic. On the other hand, dismissive comments will teach your child that their feelings are incorrect. Even if you don't understand why they're upset, it's better to validate their feelings and show empathy. If your child is crying because you told them they couldn't go to the park until they cleaned their room, tell them, "I get upset when I can't do what I want." It's challenging to keep working when I don't want to." When your child sees that you understand how they feel on the inside, they will feel less compelled to show you how they feel through their behavior. So, rather than scream and cry to show you how angry they are, they will feel better if you make it clear that you already understand how upset they are.

Guiding Children as They Identify Feelings

Children, like adults, have complex feelings. They experience frustration, excitement, nervousness, sadness, jealousy, fear, worry, anger, and embarrassment. However, most young children lack the vocabulary to express their emotions. Instead, they express their emotions in other ways. Children can express their emotions through facial expressions, body language, behavior, and play. They may sometimes express their emotions in physical, inappropriate, or problematic ways. Children begin learning the emotional skills required to identify, express, and manage their feelings the moment they are born. They learn how to do so through social interactions and relationships with significant people in their lives, such as parents, grandparents, and caregivers. As a parent, you have a critical role in helping your children understand their emotions and behaviors. Children must be taught how to manage their emotions positively and constructively.

Pay attention to cues - It can be challenging to identify feelings at times. Look at your child's body language, listen to what they're saying, and observe their behavior to get a sense of how they're feeling. Understanding what they are feeling and why they are feeling allows you to assist them in better identifying, expressing, and managing those feelings.

A feeling accompanies every behavior - Try to comprehend the meaning and emotion underlying your child's behavior. Once you understand what is causing the behavior, you can assist your child in finding other ways to express themselves.

Name the emotion - Give your child a label to help them name their emotions. Naming feelings is the first step in teaching children to recognize them. It enables your child to develop an emotional vocabulary, allowing them to communicate effectively.

Be a role model - By watching others, children learn about emotions and express them appropriately. Show your child how you feel in various situations and how you deal with those feelings.

Encourage praise - Laud your children when they talk about their feelings or express them appropriately. Not only does it demonstrate that feelings are normal and that it is acceptable to express them, but it also reinforces the behavior, making it more likely that they will repeat it.

Calming an Anxious Child

Anxiety is a normal stress reaction and can sometimes be beneficial to children. Anxious thoughts cause the brain to send out a warning signal of impending danger. When a child begins to cross the street without looking, for example, and an oncoming car is in the child's path, the anxious response signals the child to step back to the curb. However, anxiety can become excessive in some children and interfere with everyday life. Anxiety can make it difficult for children to interact with peers and form friendships, separate from parents to attend a school or other activities and learn. It can also hurt their sleep, eating habits, and physical health. Because every child is unique, the best strategy is to assist children in developing a toolbox of coping skills. While one calming technique may be effective for one child, it may not be effective for another. Building coping skills takes practice, and it's always a good idea to start by asking your child to close their eyes and name three things that make them feel calm. Children know what they need or what soothes them most of the time, but they don't know where to start.

By reframing their thoughts and using self-talk to feel empowered. While it may seem strange for children to talk to themselves at first, assertively voicing their concerns helps children gain control over their anxious thoughts.

Self-talk practice is simple and enjoyable for children. To work on bossing back those pesky worries, take the following steps:

Hug and Sympathize

We sometimes underestimate the power of the human touch. Physical touch increases oxytocin, a feel-good hormone, and cortisol, a stress hormone. A long hug can help calm an anxious child at the moment. It perfectly normal for kids to feel stressed and anxious, and anxious children need to hear this often. Whisper empathic statements, hug your child tightly and wait for the physical symptoms to subside. Once your child is calm, you can also discuss how hugging yourself or holding your hand (by clasping your hands together) can help you control the physical symptoms of anxiety.

Deep Breathing

When children are anxious, they are often told to take a deep breath, but learning to use deep breathing effectively takes practice. Daily deep breathing, mainly when children are calm, teaches them to control their breathing independently. Deep breathing will slow their heart rate and regulate their physical responses to anxious feelings when they are anxious or stressed.

Parenting an Angry Child

Parenting an angry child can be difficult. Anger can be a powerful emotion. You may be concerned about your child's anger-related behavior problems. Or, you may worry that your angry child has something "wrong" with them. Your anger may also be eliciting strong emotions in you, making it difficult for you to be the parent you want to be. "Why is my child always so angry?" You may be wondering. The truth is that a child's anger can be caused by a variety of factors. Let's take a look. Learning difficulties are a very common cause of anger in children. Whether a child has a learning disability like dyslexia or is simply struggling to keep up in math class, they can experience a range of emotions. Kids are frequently overwhelmed, frustrated, embarrassed, and perplexed. Also, children who have experienced trauma, whether through violence, neglect, or abuse, frequently struggle with anger. Trauma can influence the brain by interfering with normal emotional development. Children who have experienced severe or long-term trauma frequently respond with angry outbursts that appear developmentally much younger than they actually are. Anger could also be a result of hormonal development in a child. When children undergo puberty, anger and irritability are frequently one of the first signs that a child's hormones are taking over. This is very common in children aged 10 to 12, as well as on and off throughout adolescence. Below are some things you shouldn't do when dealing with an angry child.

Do Not React with Rage or Yelling

The first and most important rule is that responding to anger with more anger is never helpful. Adding your own rage to the mix only adds fuel to the fire. If you have difficulty controlling your own anger, it is critical that you work on developing calm-down skills. Modeling calm responses can go a long way toward teaching your children how to manage their own anger.

Address the Behavior, Not the Emotion

It's important to remember that anger isn't always a bad thing. It is an emotion that serves an important purpose. Shaming a child or attempting to suppress their anger will have an unintended consequence. Everyone gets angry from time to time. Instead of punishing anger, address the undesirable behaviors that result from it. When addressing the behavior, you can be very direct by saying something like, "I understand that this situation has made you very upset and angry. It's fine to be angry, but when you started yelling and throwing your toys, your actions were dangerous. I'm going to make you pick up all of the toys you threw to teach you not to throw things when you're angry."

Never Engage in Physical Activity

Parenting an angry child can cause a lot of stress and intense emotions. When your child is angry, it may be tempting to spank or get physical with them in order to calm them down. Using physical force on an irate child can have serious consequences. This is especially true when used in an emergency. Using physical violence, including spanking, in these situations teaches children that physical violence can be used to deal with their anger.

Motivating A Sad Child

Children appear to have a greater enjoyment of life than adults, but this does not imply that it is all fun and games. Kids can be sad at times, and it's your job as a parent or guardian to figure out what's wrong and make your child feel better.

Pay Close Attention

It will not suffice if you continue to nod your head whenever they speak. Demonstrate to them that you have a good level of understanding with them. Use affirming phrases like "I understand." "Go on," you can make them elaborate their thoughts or emotions. These minor details are important to your child. It makes them feel more at ease discussing their problems with you. Once they have gained their trust in you, they are unlikely to conceal any further problems from you.

Demonstrate Empathy and Support

To deal with a dissatisfied child, you must learn to empathize with their concerns. It is not enough to demonstrate your comprehension. Demonstrate that you understand their disdain and frustration. Emotional and physical presence are essential tools for developing a strong parent-child bond. Never be afraid to communicate with your child in any way possible. Show them your affection, love, and concern. As a result, your child will be one step closer to being content and happy in life.

Don't Try to Reduce Their Feelings.

If your child is going through a difficult time, it's crucial that he feels validated in his feelings. This begins with how you initiate conversations with your child and extends to how you respond when he tells you something is wrong. Allow your child to express himself about whatever is bothering him. Even if it's difficult for you to tell him about it, it's critical that you listen and respond honestly and affectionately. Never tell a child (or anyone else) to "snap out of it," "cheer up," or "pull themselves together." Saying these things to your child may send the message that his feelings are unimportant.

Chapter 10: Building Self-Esteem

Self-esteem is crucial as it gives an individual a feel-good vibe and confidence even in the face of difficult situations. A child with self-esteem feels proud of what he can do and can also cope even when he makes mistakes. On the other hand, children who have low self-esteem doubt their ability and feel that people won't accept them even when they try their best. Previously, we discussed building your child's emotions, and in this chapter, we will be discussing how to help your child build his self-esteem and grow into a confident adult.

Building the Courage

Courage is a learned behavior, and parents need to know that by teaching their children how to be courageous, they are equipping them with the necessary tools to survive and thrive in the face of any situation. Courage can be taught, learned and built upon over the years until it becomes habitual. When you want your child to grow into adulthood as a courageous individual, you need to teach them courage early on. If you would like to help your child master the art of bravery, then read along and see the strategies you need to implement

Teach them that bravery is manifested outwardly: Explain to your child that being brave doesn't mean one does not have an iota of fear within. A child's perception will shape his behavior and self-image. You can help a child realize that brave people are frightened too even while being brave, they only choose to override their fears; hence, they are termed brave. Also, teach your kids that courage comes in different forms. Being brave is not necessarily handling situations aggressively. For example, explain to your child that being nice to an uncool classmate in the presence of other students is a kind of courage.

Establish that you believe the child is courageous: Affirm that your child is brave as this will encourage her to reflect on her actions. Say positive words like 'you can do it, 'this is not difficult to solve,' 'you don't do things like a mediocre, I respect your choices. 'At times, your child might act difficult; try to work on these affirmations irrespective of the situation.

Please don't be too overprotective: Most parents want to shield their children from all kinds of situations, even when it is not severe. In such circumstances, the child tends to fail, as the child has been subjected to being timid. Give your child permission to mess things up. It's okay to fail, but it's not okay to stay at that point without progressing. Your child needs to know that every time they fail, they need to keep trying until they can find the right approach to come out of that situation. Similarly, don't encourage flawless bravery. Make your child know that it is okay to hang back to find a successful approach to tackle a difficult situation.

Be a role model: parents need to portray values they wish to see in their kids as there are chances that your child will want to emulate your character. Share stories of how you were in a difficult situation that made you so nervous and how to take a bold step and emerge victoriously. Your child will want to do the same when she is in a difficult situation.

Make your child try new things: Trying new things should be a regular part of your child's life. Prompt your child to try out new activities whether he will be good at them or not. For example, try new sports, art, music, new food or even new locations to have a sense of adventure.

Guide your child to make personal decisions: Do not hesitate to let your child make their own decisions as long as it won't hamper them. Don't try to be overprotective by controlling your child's choices. Instead, teach your child to use her gut instincts, as this is one way to help a child become courageous.

Developing Empathy

Empathy is the ability to emotionally understand or feel what other people feel; the capacity to imagine yourself in place of other people and see things from their point of view. Parents can help their children get empathic. Although this is a very complex skill to develop, it is not impossible. You can help your child imagine what response is comforting and appropriate in a particular situation. Empathy is the foundation of all relationships, for loving others well and even having professional success. So how can parents cultivate empathy in their children? The following are steps given by researchers and approved practitioners to build up a child's empathy.

Show your child and other people empathy: whatever you want your child to become, you can model it before them. A child can learn empathy from how you treat him and relate with others. When you show your child empathy, they trust you and feel secure with you. How do you empathize with your child? It takes many forms. It could mean understanding and respecting their personalities, being concerned about their physical and emotional needs, picking genuine interest in their lives, showing up for them whenever they are doing things that interest them. Children also take cognizance of how we treat other people. They'd watch how you treat the housekeeper like they are irrelevant, how you treat the mail carrier like a nonentity, and how you shout at the server at the mall. You can't expect your child to do any better than what they see you do. Importantly, we must try to know why we are not empathetic at times. Did you have a bad day at work? Are you stressed or tired? If you can know all this information, you'd be able to act right consciously.

Please help them see helping others as a priority: you need to constantly remind your kids that caring for them should be a top priority. Then, as parents, you can make your children participate in community development programs where they would be involved in activities that benefit people within the community. This will open them to opportunities to practice empathy.

Teach your children to manage their feelings well: Some children often don't express empathy, not because they don't possess it. You can help your child get rid of his negative feelings like anger, envy, jealousy, shame, amongst others. Such negative feelings tend to block their empathy; therefore, they would release their empathy when you help them get rid of it.

Extend the child's circle of concern: Most parents teach their children how to love one another and care for and nurture every other member of their family. While this is good, it is also crucial to teach your child to be kind to different people. Therefore, it is expedient to model a kind attitude towards different people.

Milestones in Empathy

It is crucial to develop a child's social-emotional skills, especially when they are at the early stage of their life. There are crucial milestones in empathy, and some of them are:

- You should help your child understand you; otherwise, there's no way he can understand other people. As parents, you need to establish a strong, secure and loving relationship with your child as he grows, as this helps them while they're relating with others.

- When babies are six months old, they start using social referencing. At this stage, the child is already developing consciousness of how their parents react to people and situations.

- At 18-24 months, a toddler is already developing a theory of mind. At this stage, a child realizes that he has his feelings, thoughts and goals and also others have their ideas and thoughts which may be quite different from theirs.

- At 24+ months, a toddler recognizes himself in a mirror. This means that at that age, a child understands that he is a separate person.

Killing the Mentality of Being a Victim

A victim mentality is an acquired personality trait. It is a self-destructive and unhealthy attitude in which a child considers himself a victim when anything goes wrong, even when the problem or mishap is not directed to him. Such a child tends to wallow in misery instead of seeking possible solutions. For instance, a child who usually gets bullied by his peers may start to feel completely helpless and even begin to nurture the thought that all the world is against them. Similarly, when dealing with a self-entitled child, she feels she deserves better when they don't have their way. A child with a victim mentality has a dysfunctional mindset and is liable to exhibit passive-aggressive characteristics when interacting with other people. You wouldn't want your child to have that unattractive quality, would you? Therefore, it is crucial to be on the lookout for possible signs of poor attitude in your child and help them overcome them. You can't kill the victim mentality in your child if you don't know the warning signs that could indicate that your child possesses such.

Here are a few warning signs that could indicate your child has a victim mentality

Feeling Helpless: Children who consider themselves victims feel that they do not have control over their lives. They usually have negative thoughts that bad things will happen to them and that they can do nothing to help themselves. They already have the intuition that there's no solution to any possible obstacles they may encounter. For example, such a child will not speak up when he doesn't understand the instruction given by his teacher and would not ask for help when he doesn't know how to do his homework. Similarly, when such a child is being bullied by his peers, he tends to remain passive, and when this helpless attitude lingers, there are chances that the child would become victimized by other people.

Self-Pity: A child with a victim mentality usually wallows in self-pity. Such a child would always have one complaint or the other. It is either complaining that nobody likes him or saying nobody cares to please him. Instead of seeking real solutions and asking for help, such a child channels all his energy to gain sympathy.

Engage in Negative Self-talk: A victim mentality is a vicious self-perpetuating cycle. Even when the child has several positive things to celebrate in his life, he turns a blind eye to it and focuses on the few wrong things. As a result, the child virtually overlooks all the good things in his life and pays attention to the negative that would make them feel worse. For instance, a very brilliant child emerged the best in 6 subjects out of 10 for that session, but she began to feel sober that the teachers taking the other four subjects didn't really like her and would instead give her low grades even though she did well. That is a negative thought, and such a child should be taught how to celebrate their wins and work towards achieving their goals rather than blaming others.

Catastrophizes all situations: A child with a victim mentality might always predict doom and gloom. They have negative thoughts no matter how good things appear. Even when you reassure them that things will work out, they see things crumbling before them even before making any attempt. They may make some of these utterances, "My dress is going to look the least beautiful among my friends," "I am going to perform woefully in that exam," "My classmates will make fun of me during the quiz."

A tendency to blame others: When a child has a victim mentality, he is not likely to take responsibility for his own life. Everyone is at fault for whatever goes wrong in his life. Sometimes, such children might intentionally provoke other people to stir up the adverse reaction that would affirm their corrupted notion that nobody likes them. Rather than acknowledge their role in unfortunate circumstances and find solutions, they'll likely blame others.

Feeling powerless and overreacting: children who consider themselves victims feel as though everyone except them has it easier than them, so they wouldn't even attempt to try. Similarly, they are likely to be hyper-vigilant around other people, exaggerating small things as if they were big.

Helping a Child with a Victim Mentality

Most times, kids are likely to feel like they are victims of a cruel world, but it becomes abnormal when victim mentality becomes pervasive in a child. As parents, you need to help your child get out of this poor mentality, not carry it into adulthood. If your child has a victim mentality, step in to turn the situation around.

Build Up a Gratitude Pattern: Gratitude helps to overcome self-pity. To help your child come out of that victim mentality, help him see why he needs to be grateful. Spend time with your child and talk about what they should be grateful for every day. As parents, even in the face of challenges, you need to role model a gratitude attitude for your child.

Create daily gratitude rituals to help your child realize why they need to be grateful. For instance, ask your child to tell you the best part of her day, ask her to map out a section of her room to add pin notes describing what she is grateful for each day.

Kill Negative Thoughts: As a parent, you can help a child with a pessimistic outlook towards life. You can help them recognize that their negative thoughts are not accurate, pointing out that there are exceptions. For instance, if your child feels nobody likes her, remind her that you love her and point to other people that do too.

Teach a child how to handle negative emotions: Don't make your child feel like life is a bed of roses. Instead, make them realize that there might be challenges at a point in life and teach them how to face them. Of course, a child could experience uncomfortable emotions, including sadness, anxiety, anger, fear. Still, when you train such a child to have healthy coping skills, such a situation will never defeat them. School your child that emotions are pretty normal, but it is crucial to express their emotions in healthy ways that wouldn't break them. For instance, kids who can handle disappointment when they fail in their young age will not be bothered in the face of future challenges.

Teach them to find solutions to problems: A child who lacks problem-solving skills will likely approach life passively. On the other hand, a child with problem-solving skills will easily tackle small obstacles on their way and prevent them from escalating into a terrible situation.

Teach them to help others: When kids become troubled due to specific situations, they often feel they are the only ones in it. It would help if you showed your kids that several people face one form of hardship or another. Teach your children that no matter their problems or whatever they are experiencing, they can help other people. Please encourage your child to participate in general community services regularly to help them recognize opportunities to make the world a great place for all.

Get help: Sometimes, a victim mentality may signify a mental health problem like anxiety and depression. Therefore, you need to seek professional help if you think your child's negative view of things interferes with his daily life—social, school, and other activities.

Key Takeaway

Parents must help their children build courage to face every situation they may encounter in life. Also, as parents, we must build up empathy in a child and help them get rid of the victim mentality at the early stage of their life.

Chapter 11: Reward and Punishment

What should we do to discipline our children– reward them or punish them? It's a hot topic among parenting experts, teachers, and parents. But, amid a sea of studies, surveys, and research, parents are left wondering what truly works for their children. After all, each child is an individual, and no prescribed method can produce the same results for every child. The same is true for the rules of reward and punishment. These parenting approaches have advantages and disadvantages, adding to the plight of disciplining a child using either or a combination of both methods. So, which approach is preferable? According to B.F. Skinner, an American psychologist, the reward approach has more advantages. In this method, parents give a small treat to their child as a "reward" for completing a task. This task can range from doing homework to cleaning one's room or performing household chores. The rewards, like the task, can be varied and unique. Many parents believe that 'reward' in this context refers to monetary compensation, which is why the 'reward' approach has its detractors. Many parents believe that their children will only work if they are 'rewarded.'

Using Rewards to Motivate

Parenting is undoubtedly one of the most difficult jobs there is. You are responsible for feeding and clothing your children and raising and nurturing them into good people. There is no set of rules or one correct way to parent. Because every child is unique, and every parent is unique, good parenting can look different for everyone. The rewarding of a child is an important aspect of good parenting. Some parents believe that rewarding their children with their favorite toy or the latest gadget is the best way. That is not always the case. Giving a gift to your child is an example of a tangible reward. Intangible gifts, such as praise can be used to reward your children. Parents must provide both tangible and intangible rewards to prevent their children from becoming overly materialistic. A pat on the back or praise for their efforts will make your child feel good and motivated to do it again. Rewarding children do not always have to be done after completing a task. It's also important to recognize them simply for putting forth their best effort, regardless of whether they could achieve their goal.

Rewarding Behavior

You may be wondering what kinds of rewards to give to your child. First, of course, any reward should be something that your child enjoys. Otherwise, there will be no motivation to complete the task! Aside from that, any reward with learning potential is the best type of reward.

Here are some suggestions to get you started:

Praise

Everyone enjoys being recognized for a job well done, but make sure to recognize their hard work and effort, not just their success.

Money or change

Before you dismiss the idea of giving your child an "allowance," consider this: using money as an incentive is likely to help your child learn about money management at a young age. When done correctly, you can teach your child the value of saving and working toward a goal to obtain something that he or she truly desires. Teaching your child financial responsibility can have long-term benefits.

Experiences

Exposing your child to experiences that promote learning and enjoyment is one way to foster intrinsic motivation. These experiences can include anything your child enjoys, such as trips to the library, nature walks, family movie nights, cooking, baking, camping, sleepovers, and more!

Increased Responsibilities

Kids want to feel more mature and responsible. So whether it's taking care of the dog for the weekend or delivering, responsibility can be the perfect reward that teaches kids invaluable lessons!

Returning the Favor

Teach children the importance of giving back to their community by volunteering or donating goods. Volunteering and assisting others can be a lot of fun, allowing children to get out of the house and do some good. Don't be scared to develop your concepts for your child's rewards. Always choose reward systems that are appropriate for your child and fit into your family's unique lifestyle. But there's no reason to be afraid of rewards or to think they'll turn your kids into entitled kids. Rewards are not bribes, and when used correctly, you will be teaching your child to grow up with character and responsibility while striving to achieve their goals!

Why Incentive-Based Parenting is a Bad Idea

Incentive-based parenting teaches children that exhibiting the desired behavior will always result in a reward at the end. If you reward your child every time they get an "A" on a test, their desire to learn will be conditional on receiving a prize. Is this, however, a good idea? Should we, as parents, always encourage our children to behave in a certain way so that we can reward them? The truth is that 7 out of 10 parents have probably bribed their children to eat their vegetables at dinner or even promised an extra hour of screen time if they would clean their rooms. It is not something to be ashamed of; while it can be a quick fix, it is not the best way to manage behavior over time. The issue with reward-based parenting is that it teaches children that displaying the desired behavior will always result in a prize. This will eventually become a problem because your child will begin to ask what's in it for them every time you tell them to do something. This can be an exhausting process for all parties involved. Another issue with incentive-based parenting is that kids often do not develop the internal motivation needed to maintain behaviors when they see that reward is not being offered. Let's say you reward your child every time they receive an "A" in an exam; their desire to learn is most likely going to be contingent on receiving a prize. As a result, developing an appreciation for learning itself and the internal motivation to do so becomes extremely difficult for them. Internal motivation is required to overcome the most difficult life circumstances, especially when immediate gratification is impossible. So, what should you do as a parent? You have the authority to determine when and where you will use rewards with your child. Using a reward occasionally is rarely a problem. Using incentives suitably can be quite beneficial, and research backs this up. The problem, however, arises when parents become overly reliant on incentivizing good behavior in their children.

Being a parent, like most meaningful life experiences, is complicated. You are already aware of this. There is no one method of parenting that is guaranteed to work every time. If that were the case, you would not be reading this book right now. Instead, you can adjust and develop a balanced approach to parenting that is most important.

Create a Productivity Routine

We all know that routines are important for our children. And, whether they want to admit it or not, our children understand that they, too, require them. However, it is tempting to abandon routines when there is no school. Don't they, after all, deserve a break? Yes, indeed...as well as a no. It is true that during the summer, children do not require strict schedules. They do, however, require a basic daily routine. It's what will keep everyone in the family sane. Fortunately, it is possible to create a daily routine for children that is simple enough to be flexible and structured enough to work for the entire family. It will ensure that the important tasks are completed and out of the way, leaving plenty of time for fun.

Below are a few tips to note when creating a routine.

A "perfect" routine must often be changed.

Put something you like to the test for a few days after you've found it. Don't throw everything away just yet if something doesn't work!

Examine the routine carefully before concluding that it is ineffective for your children. Can some things be moved around a little? Is there anything else that needs to be done? Tweak the schedule a little, give it a few more days, and then tweak it even more until you find something that works for you.

Therefore, a changing routine is a "perfect" routine.

This last point is crucial. Life is constantly changing. As a result, our schedules are constantly changing. So, just because a routine no longer works does not necessarily imply that it was a bad routine. It simply means it's time to create a new one!

With practice, creating a "perfect" routine becomes easier.

Don't give up if it takes a few tries to find a routine that works. It takes time to figure out how everyone's rhythm works and how long things take. However, the more you create these schedules, the easier it will become.

Applying Proper Sanctioning

Choosing appropriate consequences is a critical component of shaping your children's behavior. However, choosing the right consequences for each situation—without being too lax or too severe—can be difficult, especially if you're parenting independently. If you're concerned that your current discipline strategies aren't working, it's time to reconsider the consequences you've been experimenting with. Appropriate consequences teach children that they control their behavior—even when we aren't around to nag them. They are also tailored to each child's developmental stage, so we never ask children to do more than they are capable of.

Consider the following examples of appropriate consequences at various stages of your child's life.

Infants

Infants should never be punished. However, there will be times when you wish to modify your baby's behavior. For example, let's say they're grabbing a toy from your older child's hands or throwing their spoon on the ground in an attempt to get you to pick it up—for the hundredth time! Here are some things you can do:

Modify your tone of voice: Your baby is extremely sensitive to the tone of your voice. Therefore, speak in a different, deeper tone to influence their behavior with your voice. A simple "no" combined with redirection will suffice in most cases.

Redirect your baby's attention to a different activity. This involves assisting your baby in focusing on something else. For example, give them something else to play with if they try to grab a toy from your older child's hand.

Toddlers

When your child is a toddler, you can add a time-out to your repertoire in addition to the consequences listed above (for infants).

This entails placing your child in a separate location for a few minutes, such as a special chair or steps. Time-outs do not have to be long to be effective. The trick is to refrain from interacting with your child while in time-out. For it to work, you must ignore them! Aim for the number of minutes that corresponds to your child's age. A three-year-old, for example, would be in time out for no more than three minutes.

You can also use the time-ins technique. Time-ins are similar to time-outs, just that you stay with the child throughout the time-outs period. For example, when you withdraw a child from social interaction, you stay calm with the child until the time-outs period is over. The difference between time-outs and time-ins is that a child stays alone during time-outs, but parents stay with the child during time-ins.

Preschoolers

For preschoolers, use the same techniques you used when your children were toddlers, but with a twist on the traditional time-out: Try putting play toys in time out. It will work best if the toy is only in time-out for a short period or temporary loss of privileges. Preschoolers are not yet old enough to be motivated by days away.

Teens

You'll want to focus on consequences that will matter to your teen instead of the ones you've been using up to this point. This could include restricting your teen's access to cell phones, video games, or time with friends, temporarily suspending social media or driving privileges, raising your teen's curfew, and limiting the freedoms they've earned up to this point. It is only necessary to select one consequence at a time to be effective. However, if your teen doesn't seem to understand what you're saying, it might be a good idea to write a contract outlining the types of consequences they can expect for various infractions.

Be Cautious!

It's okay to make a mistake when trying to correct your kid. However, if you've punished your child only to discover that you reprimanded them incorrectly, you're probably dealing with feelings of embarrassment and deep guilt. Of course, there's nothing right about punishing someone for something they didn't do, but the good thing about it - and yes, there is some 'good' in this situation - is that you've noticed, and you're going to fix it right away! It's always been said that we are judged not by the things we do wrong but by how we make amends when we are at fault for something. You have the ability to forgive yourself for making a mistake. That is simply a fact of life. In conclusion, Parents consider rewarding their children for a variety of reasons, the most common and compelling of which is to increase their motivation to achieve a goal. Potty training, cleaning their room, getting good grades, being nice to a younger sibling, or joining a sports team are all examples of this. On the one hand, rewarding children for achieving certain goals is frequently effective. It can help them understand what to do and make them feel acknowledged and compensated for their efforts. Parents see rewards as a way to get their children started on the path to developing good habits. And receiving rewards causes the release of chemicals in the brain that make a person feel good, so parents can see that their children are content. This makes the parent happy as well.

Chapter 12: Knowing the Difference Between Responsibility, Choice, and Freedom

In the previous chapter, we discussed rewards as a motivator for your kids and reiterated that although rewards are good, incentive-based parenting could be a bad idea. Also, we mentioned that there is a need to apply proper sanctioning when appropriate to effect good behavior in kids. In this chapter, we will study ways to teach your children to be responsible, make the right choices and give them freedom while still exercising authority.

<u>Teaching Children to be Responsible</u>

To teach your child to be responsible, you need to start by grasping the basics of responsibility. Yes, there are some complicated chores that your child cannot take up, but he can still help you with some simple tasks. Over the years, these training sessions will help the childcare for himself his society and grow into a responsible adult. So, let's dive into tips on how to help your child become responsible.

Assign tasks appropriate for their age: Give your child tasks that they can do successfully without complications. While assigning tasks, give the child clear instructions on carrying out the task. This helps your child to become independent over the years.

Give them directives: Spend time showing and telling your child how to carry out assignments. You need to explain in the simplest term how to do things.

Balance work and fun: There's a saying that all work and no play makes jack a dull boy. Make your child understand that as much as you'd like them to do their chores, you also like them to have fun when it's time. You could teach him how to manage his time well by getting his chores done before having fun.

Avoid threats: Explain to your child that they have to follow specific rules but don't threaten them. For example, when your child wants a burger, you could say I will give you a burger when you sit down.

Act what you want them to do: parents can set good examples for their kids. For example, you could show your child how to be responsible by taking care of your things and space.

How to Give Children Freedom

Most parents do not find it easy to let go of their fears and give their children freedom. Several parents would keep their kids inside when they couldn't stay to watch them. Either you see kids stay glued to the computer screen or play games at home. We can offer our children numerous things just by staying with them. The one thing we cannot give them is independence. According to Dr. Thompson, you have to be away if you truly want your kids to have psychological ownership of their achievements in life. How and when do you give children the freedom they crave? To give your children freedom, you need to consider some of these factors. First, identify the opportunities when you feel the freedom won't hamper them. Target their priorities and make sure they do things ingeniously before other fun-filled activities. Also, you may need to negotiate a compromise by making them know what you expect them to do per time and set reasonable consequences. Similarly, you need to consider circumstances and not give them freedom if you know the result will be detrimental in the end.

Don't Be Overprotective

By nature, most parents always want to protect their children. Recently, a young woman had an exchange with her neighbor, and we could tell that she was calm even though her neighbor was making derogatory remarks about her. At a point, it almost felt like she was smiling as if to say she was being praised and about to be adorned in glory. Suddenly, she burst into anger, and before we knew it, she was moving in rage towards her abusive neighbor. It only took the intervention of hefty men to curb her from striking. Do you know what happened? Her neighbor spoke ill of her son, and she went crazy. The truth is, so many parents will lose themselves to protect their children, whether it makes sense or not. But it is prevalent to fall into the trap of being too protective of our kids. Overprotecting feels good at first, but it does no good in helping the child adapt with time. When you become overprotective of your child, you only teach them the skills they need to survive. But kids also need skills they will need when in challenging situations. There are ways to help parents calm these natural impulses and help their children thrive, and we will list some of them below.

Let them leap: If you don't allow a child to leave the crawling stage to leap, how can he possibly run? The first step is to allow that child to make his first attempt. Please give them the freedom to learn and do new things. It might be tough to actualize some milestones initially, but it would be worth it in the end. Address whatever fear you have as your worries could completely discourage your child.

Admit your worries: It is usual for parents and even the child to be worried about certain things. You may want to overlook your anxiety as an adult, or it may feel like it's beyond you and throw your plan out of the window. You don't have to do all that. Instead, you and the kids can talk about your worries together. That gives your child the understanding that it is okay to worry, but that shouldn't hinder them from trying new things. Therefore, you can develop possible ways to troubleshoot the identified problems and come up with backup plans. That way, your child will be more open to learning new things and building confidence that they are strong and capable.

Allow your child to make mistakes: Learning from mistakes helps people develop a new sense of reasoning to tackle matters logically. As parents, don't just jump in to intervene in all situations. Allowing your child to make mistakes doesn't mean that you're setting them up to fail; instead, you are helping them to build problem-solving skills to help them when you are not there. If you are sure that the mistake would not cause your child any harm or lead to a devastating result, then you can step aside.

Relieve yourself of guilt: Some parents learn and think differently from their counterparts, making their parents feel shame and guilt. Many parents tend to do more than is usual for such kids, and thus, the child then feels he is different from others. Parents need to get rid of those negative feelings to make them feel better. This gives your child the chance to discover his strengths and overcome challenges. Although this can be time and energy-consuming, it is well worth it as it helps your child acquire skills that would help him navigate problems confidently.

Set clear expectations daily: Being clear about what you expect from your child daily helps them stay accountable for their actions and makes them know that you trust them to behave as expected. Setting daily rules and limits for your child goes a long way to help them maintain good behavior.

Trust Their Choices

Parents need to get to a stage where they'd have confidence in the ability of their children to make good choices. Trust is crucial when it comes to preparing our kids for adulthood. For a parent-child relationship, trust goes both ways, and as parents, you need to begin the cycle. Most times, your child wants to tell you something; listening to them at that time goes a long way to help you understand their communication styles. It is not uncommon for parents to struggle with trusting their kids. But they need your trust and support right from the get-go. You may begin to ponder when to trust your kids, so do not pause as I will share that with you.

Reasons why you need to trust your child's choices:

They show good judgment: You can trust your child's choices when you observe that they have a good sense of judgment. Starting from the way they behave at home, handling chores and homework, their choice of friends, their behavior and manners to adults and even the information they share on social media.

They are accountable: When they keep promises and honor their commitments and accept the consequences for what they say and do.

They treat people well: They treat not just their parents with respect but every other person around them, including their peers. When a child constantly challenges and negotiates, that's a red flag.

They understand and appreciate balance: They don't tend towards extremes. As a result, a child can make good choices when recognizing situations that could be risky on time and prevent their occurrence.

They adhere to rules: They are respectful of rules. It doesn't mean they necessarily like them, but they follow them to show you respect.

Giving Freedom Without Undermining Parental Authority

The ability to work out ways to give your children freedom and trust them with it can be a balancing act. Parents need to establish their authority when their kids are young by teaching them standards. When your kids become teens, you'd need to give them more freedom and hope that they have listened to your values and will follow them. You may wonder why you have to give your kids freedom without thwarting your authority as parents? Well, that's because freedom could mean getting into trouble for kids if you do not take measures to put them in check and help them deal with the consequences of their actions. Freedom could mean allowing kids to choose after-school activities, flunking several important classes and having to repeat them. The fact is, freedom isn't always fun. Excessive freedom without control can leave them feeling unsupported and thinking you don't care for them. Why do you even have to give your kids freedom? It would help if you gave your kids a level of freedom. It would be best to give them the freedom to handle each year slowly as they grow older. You need to study them to see how well they can handle small freedoms: if they can't handle it wisely, then you'd have to work with them and help them learn how to deal with the world. If you rely too much on authority or fear, kids are more likely to rebel to gain some control. Now, how can you give your kid the freedom they crave with the trust you need to know that they'll be safe? You can only achieve this balance of freedom and authority by establishing boundaries from the outset. Setting boundaries would help you feel comfortable that your child is aware of your expectations and give them the ability to self-regulate their behaviors. How do you set boundaries for kids? Let's dive into that quickly.

<u>Tips for Setting Boundaries</u>

Your whole responsibility is to ensure that your child is healthy and secure, guide them appropriately, and support them to grow into responsible adults. There are guidelines for setting boundaries that can encourage your child to develop independence.

Set boundaries early: Children are often curious, and they are excited to learn what life is outside their confinements. As parents, you need to help your kids grow within boundaries that don't inhibit them in any way. Now, this is how it works. Boundaries should change as the child advances in age. You can't set the exact same boundaries for a teen and a toddler. Allowing boundaries to change as your child grows helps such children to adapt at a rate that they can handle with maturity.

Make them know your expectations: When you set boundaries for your child, you must state why. Parents need to explain clearly to them that if they respect these reasons and meet your expectations, you'd be happy to extend their boundaries and freedom. In addition, it would help if you taught them that freedom attracts responsibilities and that failure to comply with the boundaries will attract consequences.

Let them decide their appearance: Most parents already have their taste of a good style and fashion and want their children to follow suit. Most teenagers want to explore; they have pictures in their head that makes them cringe. As such, your child's taste might oppose your own opinion of good style. It is expedient to let your kids choose as this area of their life is essential to finding out who they are. It is a period where they explore their individuality. For most occasions, they are likely to have rules regarding their dressing style, so you may need to discuss what's more appropriate for those times.

Please give them the privilege to choose their hobbies: Hobbies can help your child socialize with other kids with whom they share the same values and interests as it creates an avenue for them to create safe areas of independence and self-determination. Please allow them to decide where and how they wish to engage in their hobbies. If your child's interest involves a level of risk, then learn the possible safety tips to protect them.

Let them take charge of some areas of their lives: Children have the right to express their views to their parents. As your child grows, you need to give them complete control over some areas of their lives. There are specific issues you feel confident that they are capable and ready to take on as they advance in age. When you give them control over these areas, make it explicit. Of course, there would be several times that you won't agree with their decisions; however, commit to accepting them. Some parents are committed to homeschooling their children at home due to inappropriate information being given to them in areas like religion, sex education etc. If your child, for instance, decides that he is no longer comfortable with homeschooling, you have to respect his decision.

Please give them the freedom, rules and consequences: When you give your child freedom, it is a form of demonstration that you trust them enough to make good decisions even in your absence. Also, having rules for them keeps them in check. Please talk about the rules, why you set them and the consequences of violating them. For instance, you can permit your teenager to go out with friends and mandate him to keep you informed whatever the situation is. Such a rule makes the child understand that you care about them. The consequences also need to be reasonable and relevant to the broken rule to be very effective. And even when they break the rule, don't yell at them; instead, speak to them calmly.

Key Takeaway

You can build your children to the point where they know the right things to do and do them accordingly. Of course, training a child to be responsible is not a day job and requires your time and effort. But, at the end of the day, you can become confident to give your children the freedom to make choices because you trust them enough to do so well.

Conclusion

The most significant influence on a child's development is exerted by his or her parents. Effective parenting is very critical in determining whether or not a child will become a productive member of society. When a child receives proper love and support, they develop correctly and the right mindset about life and its challenges. Proper parenting teaches the child what to expect in life and how to deal with it. No parent should want their child to rely on anyone other than them for guidance and support. Parenting styles do not have to be strict all of the time. However, as long as the parent is consistent in enforcing the rules, I believe children will be more likely to follow them in the event of a problem. When parents attempt to be demanding, the child begins to rebel, which is when they start to have disruptive behavior.

Giving the child some trust allows them to become more responsible and mature. Allowing the child some form of autonomy is also important. It is critical that the parent is involved in their child's dating life and that the child can talk to their parent about anything. If, as a parent, you consistently give your child instructions and advice, your child will tend to seek assistance and guidance from you first. Listening reflectively, discussing emotions, establishing boundaries and structure, and balancing independence with responsibility are essential. Observe any changes in your child's behavior. If you begin to detect any changes in their behavior, be sure to keep track of their online and offline activities.

Lastly, keep in mind that your child's development is dependent on your involvement with them, no matter how old they are. As a baby or toddler, this entails physical contact and care. As your child grows older, communication about their experiences and emotions serves as a beacon to guide them to confidence.

www.ingramcontent.com/pod-product-compliance
Lightning Source LLC
Chambersburg PA
CBHW030441010526
44118CB00011B/748